Justifying International Acts

Justifying International Acts

LEA BRILMAYER

Cornell University Press

Ithaca and London

First published 1989 by Cornell University Press.

International Standard Book Number 0-8014-2278-7
Library of Congress Catalog Card Number 89-7121

Printed in the United States of America

*Librarians: Library of Congress cataloging information
appears on the last page of the book.*

*The paper in this book is acid-free and meets the guidelines for
permanence and durability of the Committee on Production
Guidelines for Book Longevity of the Council on Library Resources.*

To W.C.H.

Contents

Acknowledgments

This book profited greatly from the reactions of others. Portions were presented at workshops at the Yale Political Science Department, Duke Law School, Columbia Law School, Michigan Law School, and New York University Law School, and participants' comments helped identify difficulties with the argument. Both the Edith House Lecture at the University of Georgia Law School and the inaugural address for receipt of the Nathan Baker endowed chair at Yale were based on material from the manuscript.

In addition, several colleagues read the manuscript and offered helpful comments. Bruce Ackerman, Kent Greenawalt, Paul Kahn, Robert Keohane, Fred Schauer, Chris Schroeder, Peter Schuck, and Cass Sunstein generously read early drafts and offered advice. Lori Damrosch and Thomas Pogge shared several as yet unpublished manuscripts that were stimulating and helpful. Joseph Raz read chapter 3. Ian Shapiro, in particular, deserves thanks for both intellectual and moral support over the long haul. Oliver Avens and Timothy Macht were not only superb research assistants, but also great fun for me to sit around with and talk to. Several anonymous reviewers suggested valuable changes, for which I am grateful.

Dean Guido Calabresi arranged time off from my teaching so that I could complete the manuscript; for this I am very thankful. As usual,

Acknowledgments

the most important contributor to the project was Cathy Briganti. May she never retire! I owe many thanks to personal friends who helped me celebrate this project's ups and downs, but especially to my husband, Bill, who helps me celebrate every single day.

New Haven, Connecticut

Justifying International Acts

Introduction

Let's say that on reading the morning newspaper you are confronted by two important news articles. In the first, you learn that the CIA has been implicated in the wiretapping and burglary of the offices of a left-wing political organization in a small country in Central America. The information obtained through this maneuver was turned over to a local right-wing extremist group, a move contributing to the eventual political assassination of a left-wing candidate for president.

The second concerns a small town in the United States. In that article, you read that the FBI has been implicated in the wiretapping and burglary of the offices of a left-wing political organization. The information obtained through this maneuver was turned over to a local right-wing extremist group, a move contributing to the eventual political assassination of a left-wing candidate for president.

How are these stories different, and how are they alike? It seems fair to guess that the second story would result in a much greater domestic political scandal, perhaps threatening top levels of the current government. Would such a differential reaction be reasonable? What is the relationship between a government's activities at home and its comparable activities abroad?

This book addresses the relationship between international ethics and domestic political justification. It claims that the two are not separate areas; whenever a state exercises coercive power, in either the domestic or international arena, the issue of political legitimacy arises. To treat these subjects separately is to overlook the most important normative foundation for international law. Separate treatment impoverishes international ethics, and it also impoverishes political theory. The difficulty of the problem of political justification cannot be appreciated when one examines only the state's right to coerce its own citizens or those acting within its territory. We live in an interdependent world, in which one state's actions have implications for those outside it as well as those within. Why does most contemporary political theory largely ignore this fact?

The chapters that follow approach international law from a perspective similar to that now employed in one legal context, namely, jurisdictional analysis. That perspective, here called "vertical analysis," holds that problems of interjurisdictional exercise of power are simultaneously problems of political justification. The insight contained in this small backwater of technical legal doctrine is as pertinent to international relations generally as it is to legal cases resolved by courts. The analogous treatment of legal issues of jurisdiction illustrates that such an approach to interstate or international relations is plausible and workable. The actual argument in favor of the vertical thesis does not, however, depend on the direct applicability of the legal doctrine.

The vertical thesis contrasts with the more traditional horizontal approach, which constitutes the mainstream position on international law today. The horizontal approach builds international law on an ethics of the relations between coequal actors, namely, states. The vertical perspective builds international law on the political norms regulating the relationship between the individual and the relevant political institution. From the vertical perspective a state's actions outside its territory, and against noncitizens, must be evaluated in terms of the political justification that grants that state the right to operate domestically. It denies that the legitimacy of the bombing of an Iranian oil platform for national security reasons is qualitatively different from the legitimacy of the bombing (or burglary or wiretapping) of the headquarters of a domestic political group for national security reasons.

While contemporary international ethics is generally motivated by horizontal premises, we will see that much, if not most, international law can be successfully reinterpreted in vertical terms. Indeed, some of it can be explained more successfully in vertical than in horizontal terms. Room is left for supplementation with horizontal premises; indeed, some issues may be better seen from the horizontal than the vertical point of view. Horizontal and vertical thinking are complementary; a vertical approach neither makes horizontal analysis superfluous nor depends on its being erroneous.

There are other schools of international theory that, like this vertical approach, challenge the currently dominant horizontal position. Early international theorists were not concerned exclusively with the relations between states; and among modern schools of thought, transnationalism and international human-rights advocacy seek to expand the scope of inquiry to the relations and rights of nonstate actors. Cosmopolitanism, likewise, objects to the neglect of individuals in mainstream international law.

I examine these schools of thought in chapter 2. They show a continuing dissatisfaction with the state-centrist paradigm and in this sense offer some support for the vertical analysis developed here. What is distinctive about the vertical analysis, however, is not merely its attention to relations with nonstate actors, a feature shared with transnationalism, cosmopolitanism, and human-rights advocacy, but its assertion that all transjurisdictional relations require political justification that can and should be analyzed in terms of domestic political theory.

Political theory itself has dimly recognized its relevance to issues of international law. The discipline has not always been oblivious to the importance of national borders in theoretical analysis of political legitimacy. Several contemporary political philosophers have addressed the role of borders in domestic theory. Just as the law of jurisdiction contributes to a vertical analysis and just as contemporary international-relations theory supports the relevance of nonstate actors, so also contemporary political theory adds to the vertical thesis certain insights about the relevance of jurisdictional boundaries to political justification. The vertical thesis thus has roots in political theory as well as in international relations and law, but the entire picture has not yet been fitted together. The impact of a complete integration of political theory, law, and international relations is much greater in all three areas than either contemporary political philosophers or international lawyers have realized.

The first part of this book sets forth the basic outline of the vertical thesis. It proposes to analyze a legal concept, jurisdiction, in terms of legitimate political authority, and then to analyze international law in similar terms. In chapter 2, I compare the vertical thesis with cosmopolitanism, realism, and what has been called state moralism.[1] Next, I suggest that the vertical thesis presents some troubling challenges to traditional domestic political theory. Not only would domestic political theory under the vertical thesis reform international law but the increased attention to international boundary problems that the thesis entails would require rethinking certain aspects of political justification.

The second part examines some implications of the vertical thesis. First it responds to various possible challenges to the argument that problems of international relations are also problems of domestic political legitimacy. It then examines the implications of the vertical thesis for three areas of international law: sovereignty, the obligation of affirmative assistance, and humanitarian intervention. It contrasts the vertical reinterpretations of these issues with the implications of a more traditional horizontal approach. The book concludes with a program of specific open issues in domestic political theory that the vertical thesis renders crucial.

In his preface to *The Anarchical Society*, Hedley Bull wrote, "When still an undergraduate I was very much impressed (I now think too impressed) by the dictum . . . that 'thinking is also research.'"[2] His book, he said, reflected the limitations of an attempt to deal with the large and complex subject of international relations simply by thinking it through. The subject of international theory is at least as large and complex today as it was in 1977. It is not possible here to give either a comprehensive analysis of the history of international theory or a detailed account of particular international incidents. Fortunately, there exist both excellent historical accounts[3] and

[1]The label is taken from Joseph Nye, *Nuclear Ethics* (New York: Free Press, 1986), 30.
[2]Hedley Bull, *The Anarchical Society* (New York: Columbia University Press, 1977), x.
[3]See, for example, Percy Corbett, *The Growth of World Law* (Princeton, N.J.: Princeton University Press, 1971), chap. 2; Walter Schiffer, *The Legal Community of Mankind* (New York: Columbia University Press, 1954).

penetrating applications of theoretical insights to particular problems.[4] These accounts demonstrate, moreover, that both history and example are theoretically exciting.

The research underlying this effort, however, is more of the sort that impressed Bull when he was a student. Drawing encouragement from a legal concept, jurisdiction, I extend its philosophical basis conceptually to two related areas. The utility of this conceptual synthesis may seem more immediately obvious to legal theorists than to political philosophers, for lawyers may already think in such terms. But the synthesis is also an invitation to international theorists and political philosophers to have their say about law. Given the cross-cultural nature of the enterprise, simply thinking it through is an adequately ambitious goal.

[4]See, for example, Michael Walzer, *Just and Unjust Wars* (New York: Basic Books, 1977); John E. Hare and Carey Joynt, *Ethics and International Affairs* (New York: St. Martin's Press, 1982).

Part I

Jurisdiction, Political Theory, and International Law: The Vertical Thesis

Introduction to Part I

Some of the most intractable conflicts in our contemporary world arise, theoretically, at the intersection of political theory and international relations. Attempts to understand them combine all of the classical philosophical difficulties concerning the proper relations between sovereign states with the seemingly insoluble theoretical issues of the legitimacy of a state's internal rule. Such situations combine the anarchy of international disorder with the immediate suffering caused by domestic injustice. They are not the textbook examples of treaty observance, diplomacy, or the proper conduct of warfare which international law traditionally has addressed. Immune to ready theoretical categorization, these disputes are tragedies of societies torn from within and attacked from without.

The possible entanglements of international relations and challenges to domestic political legitimacy seem almost endless. A few examples from contemporary world politics illustrate that when issues of international law also contain issues of domestic political theory, the resulting whole is more than the sum of its parts. A civil war in Nicaragua is more than a civil war because of the involvement of competing superpowers. Here, a conflict over domestic political legitimacy is also a conflict in international relations because both the justice of a particular domestic regime and the justice of competing international ideologies are at issue. Conversely, the application of norms of international law is made difficult by disputes over which actor is the legitimate representative of the state. The same issues arise in Afghanistan. In Panama, the military government is challenged by domestic political opposition on the grounds of its legitimacy as well as by external pressures, which the government in turn challenges as illegitimate. Why does the United States government claim a right to apply its drug laws to President Noriega or to try to topple his government?

With respect to Israel, the issues go beyond external involvement in domestic disputes to a state's assertion of territorial control divorced from the conditions of domestic justice. An international action—annexation of territory—casts doubt on the legitimacy of coercion of the individuals residing in the territory. This question cannot be understood either as simply one of international law or as simply one of domestic justice. It does not fit precisely in the domain of international law because a major claim of Palestinians is the right to political and civil liberties. It likewise does not fit precisely within the domain of domestic justice because the claim is more than a claim for political and civil rights within the framework of the state of Israel. An additional complication is the disputed status of one of the participants, the Palestine Liberation Organization, which is claimed in some quarters to have no right to represent anyone.

At the intersection of international legal theory and political theory, both disciplines have been relatively silent. Perhaps political theory has been reluctant to see itself as an applied science. A discipline whose central focus is the argument over what would constitute an ideal state is likely to be unconcerned with questions such as whether to recognize the PLO or how to choose between the Sandinistas and the contras. Political theorists tend to focus, moreover, on classical problems in the relationship between the individual and his or her own state rather than on principles that might answer questions such as: Which state is my state? What are my rights and obligations regarding other states? Political theory typically neglects such international issues—delegating them to international law, perhaps—and restricts its attention to purely domestic questions that add little to debates about current international relations.

International relations theory, by the same token, shows little interest in requiring domestic justification of international coercion. Until recently, the standard operating assumption of modern international relations theory was that one sovereign state did not inquire into the domestic legitimacy of another. Nor did it inquire into the political legitimacy of its coercive relations with noncitizens. There have been definite theoretical advances with respect to international human rights, but the potential relevance of political critique is more general than the human-rights focus on genocide and torture. Because of their respective focuses, neither traditional international law nor traditional political theory examines the legitimacy of state coercion that extends across international borders. Such coercion is not the domain of domestic political theory, for that discipline examines the relationship between a state and its citizens acting in its own territory. Nor is it the domain of international law, which examines the relationship between states.

Though examples from contemporary international relations suggest the relevance of political theory to international affairs, there is no tradition of fitting the two subjects together. Few scholars have argued that political justification is relevant to transborder activities, and few international lawyers have raised the general question of the relevance of domestic political legitimacy. There are some particular contexts in which the connection has been made, such as transnational distributive justice and international human rights. However, a general theory about how to bring arguments about political justification to bear on coercive actions that cross international borders has not been advanced.

The simplest, most direct, connection between political theory and international relations lies in the recognition that governmental coercion that extends across international borders is governmental coercion nonetheless. As such, it is subject to the same requirement of political justification as the state's coercion of its own citizens. The fact that an activity lies at the intersection of international law and political theory does not exempt the activity from the legitimacy requirements of political theory. For state coercion across a border to be legitimate, there must be the same sort of justification that would be sufficient to allow the state to coerce domestically.

This suggestion may be somewhat counterintuitive even to those who have already recognized that political theory and international law are not wholly separate enterprises. It raises a serious challenge to the legitimacy of a state's coercion of foreigners, because foreigners typically lack the sort of connection to the state that might be thought to justify its coercive power. Foreigners typically are not permitted to vote; nor have they in most cases consented (expressly or implicitly) to state coercion. One specific sort of interstate coercion where this connection has been recognized (to some degree) is a state's attempt to coerce noncitizens through judicial proceedings. In this "jurisdictional" context, the legal issue of the state's right to coerce is in reality also an issue of political justification.

Jurisdiction, political theory, and international law seem closely linked, but the precise linkage is far from clear. Each of these topics is itself a source of controversy. The foundations of international law are highly controversial, as are the principal axioms of political theory, and only a handful of political philosophers have done much foundational thinking about jurisdictional boundaries at all. Perhaps, in fact, the links between these three areas are unclear in part because the various components are not clearly understood.

But on the other hand, maybe the individual areas are unclear because the interconnections are misunderstood; it is possible that it might be easier to understand the three in conjunction than in isolation. In particular, focusing on jurisdiction (the least studied of these topics) might shed light on the other two, which have been studied intently but might profit from a fresh perspective. Our opening chapters therefore ask: What is jurisdiction? What is its relationship to international law and political theory? And what does this relationship tell us about the philosophical foundations of those two subjects?

Chapter One

Political Legitimacy and Jurisdictional Boundaries

Even within a single domestic legal system, there are many types of jurisdiction. In the American system, adjudicative jurisdiction is the power of a court or administrative agency to resolve cases between individuals. This type can be broken down further. States apportion authority among their own courts according to the dollar amount in dispute or the subject matter of the dispute, and also between the trial and various appellate stages. Externally imposed prohibitions, such as federal constitutional and statutory law, also define a state court's jurisdiction. For example, state courts may not adjudicate controversies lacking any connection with the state[1] or controversies lying within the exclusive jurisdiction of the federal courts.[2] The adjudicative jurisdiction of federal courts is similarly regulated by statute and the Constitution. But even with so many different applications, adjudicative jurisdiction does not exhaust the range of jurisdictional issues. There is also legislative jurisdiction, or the right to apply one's rule of law. And there is the jurisdiction of administrative agencies to regulate. And enforcement jurisdiction of the executive branch. All of these concepts are linked by common usage under a

---

[1]See, for example, International Shoe v. Washington, 326 U.S. 310 (1945).

[2]For example, federal courts have exclusive jurisdiction over patent and copyright cases. 28 U.S.C. 1338.

single rubric, jurisdiction, and differentiated from related concepts such as venue.[3]

Other legal systems have analogous, or partially analogous, concepts. Adjudicative and legislative jurisdiction are important both in the internal law of other countries and in international law. These uses of the concept of jurisdiction, varied as they are, do not exhaust the meanings of the term. Whenever authority is apportioned, delegated, or divided, jurisdictional reasoning comes into play. To appreciate the breadth of the concept, one should look beyond traditional states and nation states to other types of political entities. A religious authority such as the Catholic church has limits on its jurisdiction. Although I frequently use the words *state* and *sovereign* below in their usual senses, they can also be understood to include such entities.

Jurisdiction and International Law

I should note at the outset of this discussion of international law that in using the term *law* I do not intend to take a position in the age-old dispute over whether international law is "really" law. There is no particular reason to get involved in what is, for our current purposes, hardly more than a semantic distinction. The term is used here merely to refer to that body of principles that purports to regulate nation states in their international relations. Whether it is really law or not, I will refer to it as such below.

Traditionally, international law has used the concept of jurisdiction in two related areas: public international law and private international law. Private international law concerns the apportionment of authority between nations in the context of traditional private disputes. For example, in a garden-variety contract dispute it may be necessary to determine which nation's law governs the private rights at issue. Public international law, in contrast, concerns disputes between states themselves, such as boundary disputes or competing claims to resources in the deep seabed. There are also, of course, many dis-

[3]Venue is a limitation operating within a unified court system, such as the federal trial courts, which is not based on limitations of political theory but on convenience in holding the trial.

putes with both public and private aspects. For example, if one state confiscates the property of another state's nationals, both private rights of property and rights of states in relation to each other are involved. In all of these, jurisdictional reasoning is relevant because power must be apportioned among nations.

As such distinctions suggest, the legal problems dealt with under the rubric "jurisdiction" can be highly technical. Viewed from this legalistic perspective, jurisdiction is a predominately doctrinal and conceptually intricate tool of the international lawyer's trade. But this perspective is only part of the story. Jurisdiction is, essentially, the apportionment of power, and in international law power affects national sovereignty. While the concrete manifestations of questions of sovereignty can be technical, broader philosophical issues are at stake, and perhaps for this reason a variety of international legal issues have attracted the attention of political theorists and philosophers. Their analyses are not always couched in jurisdictional terms, yet the jurisdictional implications are evident:

> An American corporation owns a manufacturing operation in a third-world country. Although the plant conforms to local regulations, it does not meet American worker-safety standards. Should the U.S. government attempt to impose its standards on such enterprises? If workers are injured, should they be able to sue in American courts? To obtain the remedies provided by American law?[4]

> The dictator of a Central American nation is thought to be involved in operations distributing drugs within the United States. Can he be indicted for violation of American drug laws if he did not engage in criminal actions within U.S. territory? Would kidnapping him and bringing him to the United States for trial be legitimate?

> A human-rights violation is committed against a noncitizen in his home state by his own government or by a terrorist group. Can the noncitizen bring a private damage suit in U.S. courts?[5]

---

[4]See, for example, Henry Shue, "Exporting Hazards," in Peter Brown and Henry Shue, eds., *Boundaries* (Totowa, N.J.: Rowman and Littlefield, 1981).

[5]Compare Tel-Oren v. Libyan Arab Republic, 726 F.2d 774 (D.C. Cir. 1984).

What these issues have in common is that each turns on questions of the proper reach of a state's authority, whether it can be extended to certain areas that have strong connections with other states. These issues of the scope of state power are issues of jurisdiction.

International law has for centuries attracted the attention of philosophers.[6] One reason for the subject's fascination is probably its high drama. The perennial theme is power; the perennial topics are war and peace, sovereignty and imperialism, equality and domination. Despite the drama, the legal issues themselves seem highly technical. To address a problem of international relations in terms of jurisdiction is to transform the problem into a technical legal question. This apparently technical question of jurisdiction turns, however, on the existence of legitimate authority. To say that there is jurisdiction is to say that there is authority to act. But to equate jurisdiction with authority does not in itself advance things very far, because authority is a complex notion consisting of at least two things: power and legitimacy.

Constituting Political Theory

The constituting political theory of a state is the theoretical justification that gives the state the right to govern. The link between authority, legitimacy, and power is a product of this theoretical justification. There are two parts to the link: the connection between authority and legitimacy, and the connection between authority and power.

Political authority implies legitimacy; political authority exists only if a political theory recognizes the sovereigns' right to rule. To say that an actor has authority implies that the actor's decisions are backed by more than naked force. H. L. A. Hart pointed this out in his critique of Austin's jurisprudence, noting that many types of orders backed by force are not considered law.[7] For instance, a mugger might order a victim to hand over his or her wallet, but even if

---

[6]A good historical account is Walter Schiffer, *The Legal Community of Mankind* (New York: Columbia University Press, 1954).

[7]Herbert L. A. Hart, *The Concept of Law* (Oxford: Clarendon Press, 1961), 80–88, criticizing John Austin, *The Province of Jurisprudence Determined*, ed. Hart (London: Weidenfeld and Nicholson, 1954).

the victim complies, the mugger's instructions would not be thought of as law. Of course, a long-term ability to enforce one's will might in some cases amount to establishment of some right to rule. But that right would have to derive from some political theory about long-term de facto exercise of power. This definition is different from equating simple possession of power in particular cases with the authority to decide. The observed fact of power gives rise to authority only because some normative theory justifies the latter in terms of the former.

Political authority also involves power. The constituting political theory deals with power because the exercise of power is what the constituting political theory justifies. What distinguishes political theories from moral, epistemological, or scientific theories is that political theories specify proper purposes and methods of political coercion. I am using *political* broadly here, just as I use the word *state*, to apply both to traditional political states and to certain other structures. Not every theory of justification is a political theory, and the distinctive feature of political theory is some form of coercion, either explicit or lurking in the background. What exactly makes an exercise of coercive power political is a difficult question, one to which we will return in chapter 4. For present purposes, we need only state that coercion of some sort is central to political theory. The coercion may only amount to a power to expel an individual (such as an illegal immigrant or asylum seeker), but such power still differentiates political systems from other decision-making structures. For example, a scientist makes decisions but does not "enforce" them coercively. Individuals make moral decisions about the proper course of conduct, but putting those decisions into effect does not constitute "enforcement." When coercion and justification coincide, we can speak of a constituting political theory, and of authority and jurisdiction.

Some simple legal examples will illustrate how political theories create jurisdiction. In *Blackmer v. United States*, the government sought to subpoena as a witness a U.S. citizen that was living abroad.[8] The witness responded that he had no obligation to return to the United States to testify, since the subpoena power could not reach

8Blackmer v. United States, 284 U.S. 421 (1932).

beyond the territorial limits of the country. The Supreme Court upheld the attempted exercise of governmental power on the ground that citizens of the United States owed obligations to their government. Although theoretically unsophisticated, the reasoning was not too different in its object from theoretical attempts to explain why citizens have obligations to serve in the armed forces or pay taxes when they object to the government's military policies. This problem, of conscientious objection, is a classic issue in the literature of political theory. A successful justification for imposing obligations on citizens supports a holding of jurisdiction over Blackmer.

In a similar vein, the Court traditionally approved what is known as "transient" jurisdiction.[9] Transient jursidiction provides for serving process on an individual who is temporarily present in a state but may have no other connection with it. One well-known case involved an individual who was served with judicial papers during an airline flight over a state.[10] Whether transient jurisdiction should still be considered constitutional or not is open to dispute; since 1945, when the Court's approach to adjudicative jurisdiction changed radically, there has been no Supreme Court precedent directly addressing the subject.[11] For present purposes, the interesting thing about transient jurisdiction is its similarity to Locke's argument that even "walking upon the highways" amounted to acceptance of an obligation to obey or support the government.[12]

Other Supreme Court cases delve somewhat deeper into the question of the state's right to exercise coercive authority. *Blackmer* simply posited the state's right to coerce its citizens, and transient jurisdiction merely posits that physical presence in the state justifies political authority. But when prodded into elaboration, the Court has used language reminiscent of well-known accounts of political obligation. For example, one theory that the Court has used in upholding assertions of state power is consent. Consent may be explicit, as for

[9]Although it was merely dictum in that case, Pennoyer v. Neff, 95 U.S. 714 (1877), is usually thought to support transient jurisdiction.

[10]Grace v. MacArthur, 170 F.Supp. 442 (D. Ark. 1959).

[11]*Pennoyer* has been largely superceded by later cases such as International Shoe v. Washington and Shaffer v. Heitner, 433 U.S. 186 (1976). But see New York v. O'Neill, 359 U.S. 1 (1959), which suggests that mere presence is enough for the basis of some coercion; *O'Neill* involved the right of the state in which the individual was present to compel him or her to go to another state to testify.

[12]John Locke, *Second Treatise of Government*, secs. 119–21.

instance where an individual agrees in advance in a contract to be subject to the state's exercise of adjudicative or legislative authority. This consent-based rationale for submission to authority is one of the most strongly established foundations for jurisdiction.[13]

Consent has also figured in justifications of jurisdiction in cases in which the defendant has not explicitly agreed in advance. In such cases, the consent is "tacit"—a rationale quite familiar to political philosophers.[14] For example, the Court has invoked theories of hypothetical or tacit consent where a state law holds that driving an automobile into the state constitutes consent to suit in the state, and the driver is deemed to have appointed the forum's secretary of state an agent for service of judicial process.[15] Though the Court is no longer inclined to phrase jurisdictional results in these terms, such assertions of jurisdiction are still considered valid.[16]

On abandoning the tacit consent language, the Court moved to a theory of "fair play and substantial justice," a phrase strikingly reminiscent of Rawls's explanation of political obligation in terms of "fair play."[17] In expanding on this rather vague formulation, the Court has stated that it is fair to impose obligations on an individual who has purposefully availed himself or herself of the benefits of forum law.[18] This "benefits" rationale, coupled with a requirement that the receipt of benefits be "purposeful," has precise analogs in the literature of political obligation.[19] In the case law, it is an important element of the decision whether a state has jurisdiction to impose

[13]National Equipment Rental v. Szukhent, 375 U.S. 311 (1964).

[14]A general discussion of tacit consent can be found in A. John Simmons, *Moral Principles and Political Obligations* (Princeton, N.J.: Princeton University Press, 1979). See also Locke, *Second Treatise*.

[15]Hess v. Pawlowski, 274 U.S. 352 (1927). See also St. Clair v. Cox, 106 U.S. 350, 356 (1882).

[16]For a more recent use of consent which was implied by the party's failure to object, see Phillips Petroleum v. Shutts, 472 U.S. 797 (1985).

[17]International Shoe v. Washington, 316. The "fair play" theory of obligation is discussed in John Rawls, "Legal Obligation and the Duty of Fair Play," in Sidney Hook, ed., *Law and Philosophy* (New York: New York University Press, 1964), and Herbert Hart, "Are There Any Natural Rights?" *Philosophical Review*. 64 (April 1955).

[18]This theory was originally set out in Hanson v. Denckla, 357 U.S. 235, 253 (1958).

[19]See, for instance, Robert Nozick, *Anarchy, State, and Utopia* (New York: Basic Books, 1974), 94, imposing a requirement of consent, or Simmons, *Moral Principles*, 77, imposing a requirement of voluntariness.

a tax.[20] Although perhaps unwittingly, the Supreme Court has framed many of its decisions about the reach of state adjudicative jurisdiction in terms that, while simplistic, would be eerily familiar to most contemporary political philosophers.

Of course, the existence of examples in which jurisdictional reasoning relies on political theory does not prove the general point. Some more technical jurisdictional limits, in contrast, seem to have much less theoretical content. To take a particularly technical example, what is the normative significance of the requirement that for federal judicial jurisdiction to exist, none of the plaintiffs may reside in the same state as any one of the defendants?[21] Is it possible that such arcane requirements are really a product of political theory?

One should not jump too quickly to the conclusion that there is no theoretical content in such limitations. Where after all does the diversity requirement come from? In part it derives from Article III of the Constitution. Since the source is also partly statutory, it incorporates notions of separation of powers of the various branches of government. Congress's right to adopt a statute on this subject arises from Articles I and III, which describe the contours of the federal court system and give Congress the right to legislate. When one persists in tracing an explanation, it becomes clear that explanations are inevitably dependent on ideas of proper political structuring. The fact that some jurisdictional limitations appear ethically arbitrary does not imply that jurisdictional reasoning is not a process of theoretical justification. The apparent ethical arbitrariness has different sources.

Critics may be skeptical of the account of a limitation's genesis simply because they reject the political theory that led to it. If the underlying political theory is rejected, then the resulting jurisdictional limitation may understandably appear arbitrary. Disagreement over what political theories are convincing does not mean that jurisdiction is not linked with legitimacy. It means only that what political

[20]See, for instance, Complete Auto Transit, Inc., v. Brady, 430 U.S. 274, 287 (1977) requiring that the tax be fairly related to the benefits provided to the taxpayer.

[21]The "complete diversity" requirement denies jurisdiction whenever some defendant resides in the same state as some plaintiff. It is a statutory criterion, first applied in Strawbridge v. Curtis, 3 Cranch 267, 2 L.Ed 435 (U.S. 1806), which is more restrictive than the constitutional requirement that some defendant be diverse from some plaintiff. State Farm v. Tashire, 386 U.S. 523 (1967).

theories are valid is controversial, and therefore what jurisdictional restrictions there ought to be is equally controversial.[22]

Some current controversies over particular jurisdictional doctrines are disagreements of this sort. One example of how differences in political theory dominate disputes over jurisdiction involves the division of adjudicative jurisdiction between the federal government and the states. Under what might loosely be termed the "liberal" Warren Court view, the purpose of federal adjudicative jurisdiction was to vindicate federal rights, especially the constitutional rights that individuals have against the government. This led to an expansive view of the jurisdiction of the federal courts, which were assumed to be more sensitive than state courts to assertion of claims regarding individual rights.[23] Jurisdictional rules were a consequence of a particular political theory. This theory of the role of the federal courts is different from the "conservative" Rehnquist and Burger Courts theory of what the federal courts are for. The conservative justification is more historically oriented and more sensitive to states' rights. It searches for its jurisdictional rules in the literal language of the text of Article III (a contractarian approach to justification) and in a historical/political theory that emphasizes decentralization of government.

We cannot make judgments about a jurisdictional scheme without a theory of political justification. To define what is within, and what without, a sovereign's jurisdiction, we carry out an analysis based on particular political premises. The analytical enterprise is normative when a critical observer evaluates the political panorama according to his or her own philosophical views. Persons who argue for or against particular assertions of state authority are critical observers of this sort, comparing observed phenomena to chosen norms. In a descriptive analysis, an observer merely asks whether existing institutions make sense given some posited set of assumptions. The analysis is

---

[22]For an interesting discussion of some ways that political theories of federalism may influence jurisdictional doctrine, see Ann Althouse, "How to Build a Separate Sphere: Federal Courts and State Power," *Harvard Law Review* 100 (May 1987): 1485.

[23]See, for example, Burt Neuborne, "The Myth of Parity," *Harvard Law Review* 90 (April 1977): 1105, promoting the idea that federal courts are superior enforcers of federal rights.

descriptive in that the observer need not believe—or disbelieve—those political assumptions.

But whether one brings one's own assumptions to bear or tries to assume the standpoint of some posited political theory, perspective is a crucial element in an analysis. The concept of jurisdiction does not itself supply a perspective; it requires, however, that one exist.

Jurisdiction and Ethical Relativism

While any particular conclusion about whether jurisdiction exists must be relative to a particular set of political premises, a general theory about jurisdiction need not tie itself to any one political justification. To say that there is jurisdiction in a specific case is to say that the relevant constituting political theories grant authority to act. But to speak of jurisdiction in general is to address the relations between political theories, generally, and the patterns of coercive authority they generate.

The vertical thesis incorporates such a general approach to the problem of legitimate coercion in the interstate or international setting. The vertical thesis holds that whether a state has the authority to act in some particular interstate or international context must be analyzed by reference to the constituting political theory that grants it authority to act domestically. The vertical thesis itself does not supply such a domestic theory of political justification. It merely asserts that whatever theory is used domestically is relevant also internationally.

Under a vertical approach to interjurisdictional relations, there are two possible analytical enterprises with two different sets of objectives. The first-order enterprise involves adopting some particular premises of political theory and drawing from them conclusions about the legitimate scope of state coercion in international relations. In this way, a particular model of international relations can be constructed. If the vertical thesis is accepted, then first-order analysis is what much of international normative theory would come to be about. The evaluation of the particular international activities of national governments requires making a commitment to a particular political theory and applying the theory internationally to criticize or approve those activities.

The second-order inquiry is of a different kind. It is explicitly metatheoretical. It does not adopt any particular set of premises of political theory but instead draws out the implications of the vertical thesis's consistency requirement itself. By and large, I am here engaged in this metatheoretical enterprise. Rather than create or study specific models, it attempts to derive general conclusions about the nature of international norms and the scope of legitimate transjurisdictional coercion. The generality of this second-order approach makes it more ambitious but also, somewhat paradoxically, better able to avoid the problems inherent in developing particular political theories.

This paradoxical ability arises out of the controversial nature of political theories. So much has been said, thought, and written about possible justifications of the exercise of governmental power that it is something of a relief to be able to avoid considering the merits of such issues here. Certainly the topic is of crucial relevance to the present inquiry, which examines the proper exercise of governmental power in particular cases. But it is a topic that we can for the most part assume to have been addressed satisfactorily by others. The reason, ironically, is not that one analysis has predominated over the rest as definitive. The reason is simply that we do not need to know the *content* of the solution. We can simply assume that there exist theories that affirm "the government has a right to rule because . . ." without being able to complete the sentence. Moreover, we need not assume that only one acceptable theory can be found, or pass judgment on those that have been offered. Each observer engaged in the first-order enterprise can supply individual judgments on such issues. The second-order analyst sees the whole enterprise as a strictly logical operation. Political justifications are explanatory sentences of this form, logical relations so to speak, which can be filled in to suit each critical observer's taste.

Most of the intellectual energy that has been devoted over the centuries to questions of political theory has focused on specification and defense of acceptable theories. We thus inherit a wealth of examples. Perhaps the touchstone of legitimacy is consent—whether this means ex ante or ex post should be clarified, as well as whether actual consent is required or mere hypothetical consent. Perhaps the best solution is traditional liberal democracy. Or we might look to the divine right of kings, or to technological or philosophical expertise. Perhaps the crucial element is commonality of interest between the governing and the governed: only groups sharing common historical, religious, and cultural traditions may be grouped together politically and then only under the governance of an indigenous sovereign. Or one might choose to be convinced by sheer weight of historical fact: the sovereign has a right to govern because it inherited the structure of government from an unbroken line of sovereignty over a particular territory, issue, or people. All of these examples fit the common pattern, and we can discuss issues of international legitimacy generally without choosing among them except for illustrations.

One might object at first that such agnosticism is a most extreme example of ethical relativism. The vertical thesis seems to suggest that all political theories are equally valid. Nothing could be further from the truth. It is true that the vertical thesis itself does not make distinctions between competing approaches to political legitimacy. The metatheoretical enterprise of spelling out the implications of a vertical approach, likewise, does not involve defending particular conceptions of legitimate authority. But the vertical thesis explicitly contemplates the evaluation of competing political theories. Far from declaring that all theories are equally good, it invites analysts to criticize or reject particular international actions as politically illegitimate. Such criticism is part of the first-order enterprise, however, and not the second-order enterprise. The second-order enterprise merely imposes formal requirements of theoretical consistency between domestic justification and international coercion, arguing that consistency is theoretically necessary and examining whether other second-order requirements might follow from the formal consistency criterion.

A political justification is a relationship among an actor, a subject, and a set of events or issues. It says, "this sovereign has a right to coerce this individual in these circumstances" because the individual is a member of the voting community, or some such thing. A sovereign is sovereign only if it has *some* coercive authority over *something*. This authority distinguishes the sovereign actor from the individual. But the fact that there is legitimate authority in some circumstances does not, of course, mean that there is legitimate authority in all. The constituting political theory authorizes some things but not others. The vertical thesis holds that this line between legitimate and illegitimate state action is as relevant internationally as it is domestically. While it contemplates critical evaluation of competing justifications, it refers to domestic political theory for evaluation of what constitutes legitimate authority.

Jurisdiction and Personal Morality

There are similarities between the limitations imposed on states by a constituting political theory and the limits placed on individual actors by personal morality. Both individual and state actors seem subject to a variety of ethical constraints. For example, individuals are commonly thought to have obligations not to injure one another gratuitously, just as state actors are thought to have obligations not to torture individuals or attack other states. Persons may also be thought obligated to consider the needs of others in making decisions, a procedural requirement of sorts that resembles a state's obligation to consult its citizens. As a "jurisdictional" matter, individuals also may have obligations not to intrude into the personal spheres of other individuals, just as states are obligated not to intervene in the affairs of other states. Of course, what constitutes a justified intrusion is controversial in all of these instances. The point is not to argue for the existence of particular limitations but merely to assert that limitations set by political theory may have analogs in limitations set by personal morality. Both deal with normative limits on interaction between actors, however defined.

Yet it is important to recognize some differences. An obvious one is that the content of the actors' obligations may differ. It might be permissible for a state to impose taxes precisely because it is a political entity; for an individual to do so would be extortion or theft. Conversely, individuals may be permitted to do some things that are forbidden to political entities, such as to discriminate among other individuals on the basis of political beliefs. The government, for instance, should not penalize socialists for their beliefs, even though an individual might be entitled to decide not to affiliate with them. The moral picture changes when an actor is backed by official authority, for official status both expands and restricts permissible options.

The state's official coercive power necessitates greater restrictions that compensate for its greater potential for abuse. Discrimination might be thought less defensible, for example, and taxation more defensible.

The differences between limits on individuals and limits on states involve more than differences in content of ethical restriction, however. The foundations of the limitations are somewhat different. Certain limits on political actors derive from the state's constituting political theory. Unlike individuals, states lack corporeal existence. There is always a background problem of whether some purported sovereign actually exists. In order to show that a sovereign exists and has a right to exist, a constituting political theory must be offered.

This need for theory is important for both normative and descriptive purposes. As a descriptive matter, the pattern of coercive acts attributed to the state must be theoretically linked, or they are simply the disconnected actions of some random group of human beings. Existence is a theoretical construction because states act only through particular human agents, whose actions must be theoretically attributable to a state. Theory is needed in order to create a pattern from empirical fact.

As a normative matter, even where a pattern can be established, there is always a question whether the state's actions are justified. Whether particular actions fall within the state's legitimate powers is a theoretical matter because legitimacy is a consequence of some constituting political theory. States are creatures of theory in a way that individual human beings are not. While the content of the constituting political theory will likely be controversial, the fact that one is necessary should not be.

For this reason, there are potentially two types of limitations on state power in contrast to the one type of limitation on natural persons. States are unlike individuals in that they must show an entitlement to exercise power as well as demonstrate consistency with any other limitations on their actions. Persons need only show the latter, not the former. There can be no question of their fundamental right to exist. With states, there are issues both of their right to exist and exercise power and of their right to do particular things with the power they have. Both sorts of issues give rise to limitations on what a sovereign state is entitled to do.

For this reason, the existence of limitations on states does not depend on any analogy between state and human actors. A normative limit on what states may legitimately do does not necessarily have an analog in personal morality. To the contrary, states are different from human beings precisely because there are two potential foundations of normative limits rather than one. In addition to any limitations analogous to those placed on natural persons, there are limits arising out of the limited nature of the justifications that give states the right to operate in the first place. This foundation for limitations on state power is potentially of immense importance for international relations. It means that the search for normative limits on what states may do need not depend on any analogy between official and private actors.

The vertical approach to international relations is motivated by the recognition that state actors are endowed only with limited powers. The fact that their powers are limited is as pertinent to the international context as to the purely domestic context. In both contexts, an action by the state must be evaluated according to whether it complies with the requirements of the constituting political theory. Every exercise of coercive power contains issues of political justification. Indeed, issues with international ramifications are more likely to tread close to the limits of the constituting political theory, because they are likely to be farther removed from the core of a state's legitimate powers.

To reinterpret international law as founded, at least in part, on the limits inherent in a sovereign state's constituting political theory results in a very different approach to the subject. This "vertical" perspective on international theory provides a foundation for the normative limits on state conduct different from those for existing approaches to international relations. It does not rely on an analogy between states and individuals, nor on the applicability of ethics to official conduct. Instead, it relies on the same domestic political theory that provides the state its justification for operation in the first place. Let us turn our attention, then, to the consequences of the vertical perspective for existing approaches to international relations.

Chapter Two

Political Theory and International Law

The vertical thesis holds that every action undertaken by a state must pass the test of legitimacy imposed by domestic political theory. For example, most would agree that the U.S. government would be behaving illegitimately if the party in power undertook to maintain its position by extralegal covert action against members of opposing political parties. The American reaction to the Watergate burglary certainly suggests as much. Assassinating opposing candidates would, a fortiori, also be out of bounds. What, then, of our government's involvement in political assassinations in other nations?[1] Is there any way to explain why an action suddenly becomes legitimate when it is undertaken outside one's territory? Would support for death squads in El Salvador be any different from support for death squads in Miami?

Vertical analysis imposes a consistency requirement between domestic and international norms, stating that whatever limitations are in effect domestically are also in effect internationally. Despite this consistency requirement, actions that are prohibited domestically are

[1]John E. Hare and Carey Joynt, *Ethics and International Affairs* (New York: St. Martin's Press, 1982), 155, conclude that "political assassination is not an acceptable tool for a state because it undermines the rule of law in its own jurisdiction," an apparent example of vertical reasoning.

not necessarily also prohibited internationally. The two contexts may, of course, be different in ways that are relevant to the constituting political theory. For example, if it were part of a domestic theory that the government not place wiretaps on private phone lines absent a compelling justification it is entirely possible that such justification might exist more frequently in a state's international than in its domestic affairs. All that the vertical thesis does is to require that state actions be equally consistent with normative limits on state power. Differences in how the government acts, in other words, cannot be explained simply on the grounds that one situation is domestic and one international.

The vertical thesis differs from existing approaches to international law in two respects. First, it does not focus on the relations between states, per se, but on the relations between a state and an individual. It thus differs from most traditional schools of thought, which focus on the horizontal relation between states rather than the vertical relationship of state to individual. Second, the vertical limitations arise out of political theory, not out of an analogy to personal ethics. In contrast, even when contemporary theory does move away from the horizontal paradigm, it does not evaluate state actions in terms of political theory but in terms of personal morality or ethics. As I will argue below, however, there are advantages to founding international-relations theory on the requirements of political justification; and in this respect, the vertical analysis stands on a surer footing than traditional and contemporary schools of thought.

Traditional and Contemporary International Theory

It has become fairly standard to divide traditional thinking in international law into three camps: realist, cosmopolitan, and state moralist.[2] All three are dominated by horizontal reasoning. Both the state

---

[2]The phrase is taken from Joseph Nye, *Nuclear Ethics* (New York: Free Press, 1986), 30. Comparable three-part distinctions can be found in Charles Beitz, *Political Theory and International Relations* (Princeton, N.J.: Princeton University Press, 1979); in Hedley Bull, *The Anarchical Society* (New York: Columbia University Press, 1977), 81; and in Nye, *Nuclear Ethics*, 27.

moralist and the realist take states as the relevant actors.[3] The realist denies that there are principled limitations on what states may do, remaining skeptical of purported norms of international law. The state moralist recognizes principled limitations but by and large assumes that these limits cannot be enforced by individuals because the holders of the rights are the states themselves. Both lines of thinking are horizontal because they regulate states in relation to one another. The cosmopolitan approach in contrast treats states as ethically obsolete; the relevant actors in this view would ideally be the members of the world community. This view is also horizontal because it focuses on the relations between persons, not on the vertical relations between a state and an individual. Let us examine the cosmopolitian perspective first.

It is difficult to summarize the cosmopolitan view, because there is no common creed but only a losely defined set of attitudes.[4] In contrast to the two other views, which see sovereign states as the only relevant actors in international problems, the cosmopolitan view emphasizes the importance of the individual. Thus, the cosmopolitan de-emphasizes "state interests" as reasons for acting, denying that that the good of the state, or even perhaps the state's continued existence, justifies doubtful foreign policies. The cosmopolitan maintains instead that human rights transcend national boundaries and that obligations of assistance apply to citizens of other states as well as to those of one's own. The view has been found particularly appealing

[3]For a historical discussion of the concept of states as relevant actors, see Peter Butler, "The Individual and International Relations," in James Mayall, ed., *The Community of States* (London: Allen and Unwin, 1982). Oppenheim was particularly dogmatic on this point. Lassa Oppenheim *International Law*, 1st ed. (London: Longmans, Green, and Co. 1905), 1: 4, 18. The state-centrists are described in Jenks, *Common Law of Mankind*, 8–9.

[4]For an illustrative application of cosmopolitan reasoning, see David Luban, "The Romance of the Nation State," in Charles Beitz, Marshall Cohen, Thomas Scanlon, and A. John Simmons, eds., *International Ethics* (Princeton, N.J.: Princeton University Press, 1985); Judith Lichtenberg's "National Boundaries and Moral Boundaries: A Cosmopolitan View," in Peter Brown and Henry Shue, eds., *Boundaries* (Totowa, N.J.: Rowman and Littlefield, 1981). For another view that cosmopolitanism rejects the paradigm of a "society of states," see Terry Nardin, *Law, Morality, and the Relations of States* (Princeton, N.J.: Princeton University Press, 1983), 44, 46, 272, 274.

as a justification for international redistribution of wealth.[5] National borders are ultimately not important in moral questions.

It is hard to critique cosmopolitanism because the extent to which particular cosmopolitans really carry the emphasis on individuals to its ultimate conclusion is unclear. Nardin, whose account of cosmopolitanism accords reasonably well with the one just given, therefore differentiates between utopian and more moderate cosmopolitanism.[6] Only the utopian version concludes that states are morally irrelevant; a more moderate position merely requires recognition of the rights of individuals as well as of states.

Similarly, Nye notes the weaknesses of "unsophisticated" cosmopolitanism. First, he says, "to underestimate the significance of states and boundaries is to fail to taken into account the main features of the real setting in which choices must be made."[7] International ethics, he argues, must consider political action along state lines. Second, there is in fact a potential moral dimension to national politics. A pure cosmopolitanism would improperly ignore the role of nation states in acheiving self-determination of peoples.

A vertical perspective underscores these observations about the moral and practical relevance of the nation state. If a state is indeed founded on a valid constituting political theory, then it is thereby entitled to exercise state power in the appropriate circumstances. Nation states are not, for this reason, morally irrelevant, nor, under a vertical approach, are they obsolete. An extreme cosmopolitan might consistently also be an anarchist, but it would seem inconsistent to recognize the state's domestic power to further its interests while categorically denying that a state has legitimate rights to act in the international arena. An individual not wishing to hold such an extreme domestic political position as anarchism should be willing to recognize that states, as entities, are also important actors internationally.

---

[5]For instance, a current dispute over redistribution focuses on the question of whether there is as great an obligation to members of other nations as to one's own fellow citizens. A cosmopolitan would answer in the affirmative. For a discussion of this question, see chapter 6.

[6]Nardin, *Relations of States*, 44–46.

[7]Nye, *Nuclear Ethics*, 33.

These remarks on utopian or unsophisticated cosmopolitanism may be somewhat beside the point since it is possible that no cosmopolitan would take such an extreme view (except, perhaps, a domestic anarchist). A moderate cosmopolitan, who believes in the prerogatives of both states and individuals, has a great deal in common with both the transnationalists and the human-rights advocates, and for this reason we can postpone discussion of moderate cosmopolitanism until we examine those approaches. These schools of thought are the closest of existing schools to the vertical perspective argued for here.

For present purposes we need only note that cosmopolitan tendencies must be tempered by recognition of the theoretical right of a state to operate. An extreme utopian or unsophisticated cosmopolitanism would be inconsistent with the vertical perspective. While the recognition of a state's constituting political theory would not bother a moderate cosmopolitan, it would compel restatement of at least some questions of international law in terms of the constituting political theory. A moderate cosmopolitan, who recognized a state's domestic legitimacy under its constituting political theory, should not only recognize the moral relevance of the state's existence but also differentiate between those international acts that the theory authorizes and those that it does not. Such differentiation is the core of a vertical approach.

Realists versus State Moralists

Probably more widely known is the dispute between realists and state moralists; these groups have traditionally captured center stage in the theoretical debates over international law. Both schools recognize states as the relevant actors; international law is concerned with the "society of states." They disagree, however, on whether there are principled limits on what states are entitled to do. Realists insist that there are no principled limits on a state's pursuit of its interests in the international arena, only pragmatic limitations. State moralists maintain that states are limited by principles in the same way that persons are limited in domestic problems by personal morality.

The realist tradition combines three lines of reasoning.[8] The first is that of the moral sceptic. Realists sometimes seem to be saying that there are no secure foundations for moral reasoning, especially in international law, where a single norm must deal with many different cultures.[9] The second concerns national interest. The realist is likely to emphasize that the statesman, acting as an agent on behalf of his or her nation, does not have the same freedom to be altruistic as one would have in private conduct.[10] The third holds that the most important values, peace and order, are better achieved by a diplomacy that focuses on pragmatic concerns such as the balance of power than by a diplomacy that focuses on morality.[11]

The second and third of these lines of reasoning are actually types of moral reasoning; realists who focus on these arguments for realism therefore have a somewhat different slant from those who simply claim that value judgments are impossible in international affairs. Nye, for instance, does not count moral sceptics as realists at all.[12] What links them together, however, is their common rejection of traditional principles of international law, such as respect for sovereignty of other nations and prohibitions against aggression or intervention in other states' domestic affairs—precisely the principles that the state moralists uphold as central.

The state moralists occupy what is probably the mainstream position in international law. Traditional international law makes the most sense from a state-moralist point of view. The state moralists are concerned to refute the argument that international law is not "really" law. Despite the fact that there is no centralized enforcement mechanism, they argue, the norms of international conduct constitute

---

[8]Classic examples of the realist position can be found in George Kennan, *Realities of American Foreign Policy* (Princeton, N.J.: Princeton University Press, 1954); Hans Morganthau, *In Defense of the National Interest* (New York: Knopf, 1951). See also Michael Smith, *Realist Thought from Weber to Kissinger* (Baton Rouge, La.: Louisiana State University Press, 1986).

[9]Arthur Schlesinger, "National Interests and Moral Absolutes" in Ernest Lefever, ed., *Ethics and World Politics* (Baltimore, Md.: Johns Hopkins University Press, 1972), 25.

[10]See, for example, Kennan, *American Foreign Policy*, 47–48.

[11]This was Kissinger's position, according to Nye, *Nuclear Ethics*, 29.

[12]Nye, *Nuclear Ethics*, 29.

a legal system in important ways.[13] Thus, international law is *possible* to a state moralist. Having shown its theoretical possibility even in a world with no central enforcement mechanism, the state moralists turn their attention to ascertaining what norms exist and what they require. In this way, state moralists dominate most discussions of traditional principles of international law, because they are the ones that find such state-state norms important and relevant.

Contemporary International Theory

Contemporary international theory both develops these perspectives and goes beyond them. Some of the literature continues on in the state-moralist tradition; other works examine elements of that tradition with a more cosmopolitan slant.

Contemporary state moralists address a set of problems that go far beyond the traditional concerns with respect for other states' sovereignty, diplomatic immunity, freedom of the seas, and other issues that have concerned international lawyers for centuries. Distinctively modern problems include nuclear ethics, the morality of bombing attacks that threaten the lives of innocent civilians, the obligation of famine relief in a world threatened by population explosion, the danger of international pollution—problems that have come to the forefront in the second half of the twentieth century.

Walzer, for example, has focused on the conduct of modern warfare.[14] There are clear links between his work and the study of traditional rules of warfare; indeed, he examines historical examples in the process of analyzing modern ones. Walzer is a state moralist; he recognizes both the moral significance of communities and the ethical limitations on them.[15] Nardin, similarly, in a more general

---

[13]Nardin develops this argument at length and persuasively in *Relations of States*.

[14]Michael Walzer, *Just and Unjust Wars* (New York: Basic Books, 1977).

[15]See, for instance, the discussion in Walzer, *Just and Unjust Wars*, 58–59: "If states actually do possess rights more or less as individuals do, then it is possible to imagine a society among them more or less like the society of individuals. The comparison of international to civil order is crucial to the theory of aggression. I have already been making it regularly." His "presumptive" status of states is elaborated further in Michael Walzer, "The Moral Standing of States: A Response to Four Critics," *Philosophy and Public Affairs* 9 (Summer 1980): 209.

study of international morality, falls in the state-moralist camp.[16] Like Walzer, he sees international ethics as a discipline primarily concerned with the moral limitations on the relations between states.

Some other contemporary theorists go in a rather different direction, arguing that international law cannot be limited to the relations between states. For example, pointing out that international law was not always exclusively state-centrist, Corbett stresses the need for norms to govern the relations between states and nonstate actors across national boundaries.[17] This perspective has been called "transnationalism" in order to de-emphasize the state-state aspects of disputes. Not all disputes that cross borders are between nation states; some are between a state actor and a nonstate actor or between two nonstate actors. The word *international* seems to suggest that all disputes are between nations.

This school of transnational law is associated most prominently with Jessup,[18] but also with other authors such as Bull, Jenks, Keohane, Nye, McDougal, and Friedman.[19] They seek, in part, to develop principles for dealing with important classes of modern disputes that do not really fit in the state-state paradigm. For example, international organizations such as the World Bank or the Red Cross have relations with individuals that call for legal and ethical analysis, which state-centrist international law does not supply.

At the same time that transnationalists were challenging the state-

---

[16]See, for example, Nardin, *Relations of States*, 233: "International law is a body of authoritative practices and rules constituting a common standard of conduct for states in their relations with one another."

[17]Percy Corbett, *The Growth of World Law* (Princeton, N.J.: Princeton University Press, 1971), 184.

[18]Phillip Jessup, *Transnational Law* (New Haven, Conn.: Yale University Press, 1956); see also Wolfgang Friedman, Louis Henkin, and Oliver Lissitzyn, eds., *Transnational Law in a Changing Society: Essays in Honor of Philip C. Jessup* (New York: Columbia University Press, 1972).

[19]Robert Keohane and Joseph Nye, *Transnational Relations and World Politics* (Cambridge, Mass.: Harvard University Press, 1970); Bull, *Anarchical Society*, 145, explains how contemporary international law no longer deals exclusively with states; Clarence Jenks, *The Common Law of Mankind* (London: Stevens and Sons, 1958), 14, claims that the view that international law reflects only the relations of states no longer reflects realities of international life; Wolfgang Friedmann, *General Course in Public International Law*, Hague Recueil des Cours 127 (1969), chap. 5; Myres McDougal, *International Law, Power, and Policy: A Contemporary Conception*, Hague Recueil des Cours 82 (1953), 133.

centrist orientation of traditional international law, human-rights advocates were also rejecting the dictum that international law was exclusively designed to regulate conduct between states.[20] They did so in the context of human-rights abuses. Traditional state-moralist thinking not only failed to acknowledge the importance of human rights, but it also actually stood in the way of their achievement internationally. It ignored them through its provision that only states could be rights holders under international law; the individual had no standing even to make a claim based on international legal principles. It stood in their way through its insistence on the sovereignty of the nation state, which characterized as improper any efforts by one state to cure human rights abuses in another.

These two strands of transnationalism and human-rights advocacy have some similarities to both state moralism and moderate cosmopolitanism. Like state moralists, the transnationalists and rights advocates find normative thinking about international problems to be both possible and important. Their enterprise is similar to that of state moralists in that international theory is an ethical, not just a pragmatic, discipline. But unlike state moralists, while recognizing the moral and practical importance of nation states, they also recognize the rights of individuals. In this sense, they are similar to the cosmopolitans. Like cosmopolitans, they perceive individuals and private organizations as important actors in the international arena. But unlike extreme cosmopolitans, they do not see the nation state as necessarily obsolete or morally irrelevant. These contemporary thinkers might be grouped together with moderate cosmopolitans under the heading ''transnational moralists.''

Transnational-moralist reasoning is probably the closest existing analog to the vertical perspective because it focuses on the relations between states and individuals and accords normative significance to both. It is closer to vertical reasoning than are the positions of contemporary state moralists like Walzer and Nardin, who still focus primarily on the rights of nations or communities vis-à-vis one another. The transnational moralists focus on ''vertical'' relations;

---

[20]To refer to human-rights advocacy in this way is somewhat misleading in that it seems to contrast human-rights concerns with the concerns of other authors belonging to other schools of thought. In fact, however, many state moralists, cosmopolitans, and transnationalists were extremely concerned with human rights.

indeed, some of them have characterized their thinking as "vertical" rather than "horizontal."[21] However, the gulf between transnational moralism and the vertical thesis is still fairly wide.

The reason is that, like contemporary state moralists, transnational moralists look to ethics rather than political theory for their normative inspiration. It is clear enough why state moralists such as Walzer and Nardin might rely on ethics; an international theory that concerns the relations between equals (namely, communities or states) is more nearly analogous to ethics (which addresses the horizontal relations between coequal persons) than to the norms governing the vertical relationship between individuals and states. However, it is surprising that transnational moralism approaches the subject from a horizontal point of view: it needn't. The transnational moralists, like contemporary state moralists, phrase things in terms of ethical limitations. Though they rely on vertical terminology on occasion, they do not turn to the study of political justification for their normative principles. Perhaps the closest that the contemporary literature comes to reliance on the study of political justification is in human-rights advocacy, for arguments that human rights have been transgressed resemble arguments that the government has exceeded its political justification. Yet the human-rights advocates stop short of a full vertical analysis in several respects.

First, their arguments are not abstract ones about the relationship between political theories, generally, and international theory. They do not argue that domestic and international theory should be consistent *whatever the domestic theory might be.* Although this position may be implicit in some of their arguments, it remains to be stated and developed as a theoretical tenet. Their arguments are founded instead on particular political theories, namely, those recognizing essential human rights. This is particularly true of authors that attempt to apply principles from John Rawls's *Theory of Justice* to the international redistribution of wealth.[22] It is probably the case that

---

[21]See, for example, Friedman, *Public International Law*, 93. This use of the terms "vertical" and "horizontal" should be contrasted with that of Richard Falk, "International Jurisdiction: Horizontal and Vertical Conceptions of Legal Order," *Temple Law Quarterly* 32 (Spring 1959): 295. Falk contrasts the horizontal relations of states with one another to the paradigm of states relating to a superior force such as an international adjudicative body.

[22]We will discuss such efforts in chapter 6.

most of us would find such political theories more convincing than theories that disregard human rights, and consequently one tends to agree with much that the human-rights advocates say. As a theoretical matter, however, they do not go far enough in developing an explicit link with political justification.

Second, and more important, once a general vertical thesis is adopted, it has implications for many international problems beyond those recognized as human-rights issues. For example, one typical human-rights problem involves a state that is violating human rights and another state that is considering intervening but is also aware that intervention would possibly infringe the first state's sovereignty.[23] But it should also be borne in mind that when the acting state intervenes, it must also square its actions with the requirements of its own political theory. There are two political theories involved, in other words, and not just one. There is the theory of the state that is violating rights and the theory of the one that is contemplating intervention. A general vertical analysis examines every official activity of each state.

Moreover, it might be possible to violate the requirements of political justification even without violating principles of basic human rights. The human-rights tradition has focused primarily on egregious violations of rights, such as genocide, torture, and severe denials of civil liberties. Certainly it is not a failing of the human-rights tradition that it has expended its energy on these, most pressing, problems. But that is not to say that all the requirements of political justification are necessarily satisfied by observance of human-rights norms. In addition, for instance, there might be requirements of procedural due process, prohibitions on double jeopardy, and rights to full electoral participation. Or the mere exercise of coercive power over those with no connection with the state might be illegitimate. There are political wrongs that stop short of the violation of basic human rights.

Human rights advocates are motivated, understandably, to remedy particular existing abuses. This purpose necessitates a theory that explains why protection of basic rights is an important international goal. To say that this rights perspective might be taken further, in

---

[23]We will discuss humanitarian intervention at greater length in chapter 7.

Figure 1. Vertical and horizontal relations

theory, is not to denigrate human-rights advocacy but to supply it with an additional foundation.

Responding to the Realists

That additional new foundation may in fact be more secure than the one underlying existing approaches to international law. The threshold issue of international law is whether it is possible to speak of international law in normative terms; realists typically maintain either that it is not possible or that the only normative value is pursuit of state interests. Cosmopolitans, state moralists, and transnational moralists alike must address this realist argument, and most of them do.[24]

Recognition of the relationship between domestic political theory and international law restructures the terms of this debate. At stake in this restructuring is whether international law is more influenced by political theory or by ethics. Domestic political theory has traditionally dealt with the legitimacy of the hierarchical (vertical) relationship between an individual citizen and his or her government. Why, and in what circumstances, does a state have a right to exercise coercive authority? Ethics, in contrast, deals primarily with an individual's relationship with other individuals, a horizontal relationship. The issues may be diagramed as in Figure 1.

---

[24]See, for example, Walzer's chapter "Against Realism" in *Just and Unjust Wars*. Perhaps the best descriptions of the conflict between the realists and the believers in principled limitations are to be found in Beitz, *Political Theory*, pt. 1, and Marshall Cohen, "Moral Skepticism and International Relations," in Beitz et al., *International Ethics*. An excellent historical and conceptual account can be found in Walter Schiffer, *The Legal Community of Mankind* (New York: Columbia University Press, 1954).

In the international arena, where there are competing sovereigns, the relationships may be diagramed as in Figure 2. States possess authority over their own citizens, but the relationship between states and noncitizens or other entities is unclear. There are two ways to visualize the problems of international law: as a horizontal relationship between states or as a vertical relationship between a state and a noncitizen. The traditional approaches treat international law as the former rather than the latter, although as we have seen, transnational moralists have mitigated this emphasis somewhat.

This horizontal conception of states as relevant actors goes hand in hand with greater emphasis on public international law than on private international law. The public law questions of war and peace have captured the greater part of philosophical attention, and the analogy to ethics fairly naturally prevails if international law is dominated by a horizontal public law paradigm. But even in public international law, recognizing states as relevant actors need not mean denying the importance of relations between a state and those outside—what we will refer to as "diagonal" relationships. It is relevant to ask whether the consequences of a state's foreign policy on noncitizens are justified. Furthermore, there are also important international law issues in private disputes where two or more states compete to govern the relationship between individuals. In such cases, the relationships between each of the individuals and each of the competing states (vertical relationships) are of paramount importance.

Two examples will illustrate how vertical relations are involved in both public and private international law. A standard problem of public international law is the proper treatment of noncombatants during war. Under the vertical perspective, the question would center around the right of a state to harm civilian noncitizens. With regard to

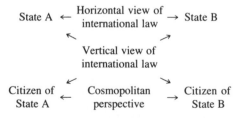

Figure 2. Vertical and horizontal relations in international relations

soldiers from another state, a justification might be based on self-defense, but the same cannot be said with regard to noncombatants. Adopting a vertical perspective does not by itself provide an answer to the question of whether a justification exists, but merely a point of view. It focuses on whether the vertical relationship legitimates coercion.

A typical problem of private international law concerns the application of local law to a transnational antitrust dispute. May the United States apply its law to a foreign corporation acting in a foreign country but causing local economic impact?[25] Again, the vertical issue must be posed. Does the United States have a right to exercise coercive power under the circumstances? Would the exercise of coercive power be fair and reasonable to the opposing party? This is a question of political theory.

Rephrasing questions in terms of the constituting political theory favors those who engage in normative analysis over the realists. The currently dominant analogy to ethics has given undue advantage to the realists; substituting an emphasis on political theory redresses that imbalance. The analogy to ethics handicaps normative theorists because it effectively forces them to rely on a vulnerable comparison of states to people. Both ethics and international law are conceptualized as horizontal relations between formal equals, and the dispute over whether there are normative limits is phrased in terms of whether there exist principled limits on states that are the functional equivalents of the ethical limits on individuals.

The usual normative argument that there are ethical limits on states is vulnerable because it rests on a comparison between two different sorts of entities. Are individuals and states normatively comparable (if they are, there should be an analogous ethics of international law) or are they so different that no analogy can be drawn? Clearly, there are important differences that realists can point to in denying that sovereign states are bound by ethical limitations as humans are. One might argue for instance that since states are sovereign, there can be no principled limitations on their freedom of action. Unlike people, that is, they are in a vertical relationship of power over other actors.

---

[25]See, for example, United States v. Aluminum Co. of America, 148 F.2d 416 (2d Cir. 1945).

This means two things. First, they are bound to further the interests of their own citizens, not the interests of outsiders. Second, there is no entity in a position hierarchically superior to them. They are, according to this argument, in a Hobbesian state of nature, unlike individuals, who are bound by legal and moral rules.[26]

The realists therefore have some strong arguments that relations between states are not like relations between people.[27] Their dispute with the state moralists then centers on whether these distinctions are important enough to warrant rejection of international ethics. This debate is transformed when international law is visualized from the vantage point of the constituting political theory. Though it remains possible that there might be limitations arising out of the horizontal relations between states, another source of principled limitations results from the restrictions inherent in vertical relations. The comparison is not between two horizontal relations (citizen-citizen and state-state) but between two vertical ones (state-citizen and state-noncitizen).[28]

This transformation is important for several reasons. First, the relationships being compared are not between qualitatively different sorts of entities. It is no longer important whether states are "like" people—whether they have rights and obligations as people do—or whether their sovereignty raises them above principled limitations from the outside. Instead, each of the relationships in the comparison is a vertical relationship. Each involves a state and an individual, a feature that seems to make the relationships more nearly comparable. The argument is not that normative principles are relevant to a state-state relationship because they are relevant to a person-person relationship but that normative theory is equally relevant to all state-person relationships.

Second, in neither of the two vertical relationships is there a hierarchically superior entity to mediate or enforce normative standards. In this sense, neither is more a Hobbesian state of nature than

[26]See Beitz, *Political Theory*, 27–49, and Cohen, "Moral Skepticism," 23–33, for statements and criticisms of these arguments.

[27]See, for instance, Schlesinger, "National Interests," 22. Bull also acknowledges the difference, although he is not a realist (*Anarchical Society*, 49).

[28]For a discussion of the importance to international law of absence of centralized enforcement, see Louis Henkin, *How Nations Behave* (New York: Council on Foreign Relations, 1979).

the other. This similarity is important because some realists rely on the absence of such a superior entity in denying that any important analogy between the two horizontal relationships exists.[29] Thus, one of the features differentiating state-state and person-person relationships, namely, the existence of a superior sovereign, is absent in *all* vertical relationships.

In both of these respects, the vertical comparison puts international law on a surer footing. The analogy shifts the burden of proof somewhat. Presumably realists, like other political theorists or philosophers, would agree that a state's relations with its own citizens should comply with principles of political justification. The exercise of coercive authority over human beings should be consistent with applicable principles of political legitimacy. But if humans are entitled to civil and political rights as a matter of political theory, why don't analogous principles regulate the relationship between a state and *all* of the individuals over whom coercive power is exercised? Why are noncitizens not entitled to the benefits of principled limits on sovereign power?

Finally, the vertical thesis poses not only a normative challenge to the realist but a descriptive one. The normative challenge is to explain why some vertical relations might be thought subject to critical scrutiny while others might not. The descriptive challenge is simply to delineate which ones are which. When the argument is framed in terms of whether the state-state relation is like a person-person relation, at least in any given case one knows which sort of relation one is talking about. But vertical relations do not fall easily into two categories, those that require political justification because they are domestic and those that do not. What if a state coerces a noncitizen who is only temporarily present? A citizen who is temporarily absent? The child of a citizen and a noncitizen, who has never been in the country or one who has never left?

The realist position artificially truncates the reach of political theory. It limits the discipline's normative impact by declaring it irrele-

---

[29]Compare, for instance, Anthony D'Amato's discussion of the lack of international enforcement mechanisms, where he points out that in domestic disputes between the individual and the state there is likewise no enforcement mechanism. ''Is International Law Really 'Law'?'' *Northwestern University Law Review* 79 (December 1984): 1293, 1300.

vant to issues of foreign policy. But the normative justification for such a limitation is doubtful. And it is not even very clear as a descriptive matter where the line might be drawn. Neither of these questions has been addressed by the international realists; their arguments are far less convincing against the vertical thesis than they are against an international normative theory that is founded on ethics. The vertical thesis takes the weakness of international ethics, namely, the differences between states and persons, and turns it into a strength, for it builds precisely on what is distinctive about states, their need for a political justification.

Possible Realist Responses

There seem to be several possible responses to this challenge. One would be to deny that issues of political justification arise in the state-noncitizen relationship by denying that a political relationship exists. It might be argued, in other words, that a state dealing with its own citizens (or with noncitizens in its own territory) is acting qua government, but that in dealing with noncitizens outside its territory it is not acting qua government. This raises a rather formidable theoretical question: What is the proper domain of political theory? What relationships are political ones that must be justified? Are some coercive actions different so that the usual requirements of justification do not apply?

An analogy might make this proposed argument clearer. Parents have special moral responsibilities toward their own children that they do not have toward others. The parent-child relationship, in other words, is governed by a special set of principles. For instance, it is arguable that I have a responsibility to help pay my child's medical-school tuition if I am capable, but I do not owe such a duty to other people's children. In the same way, it might be argued, political theory is only pertinent when a certain sort of relationship exists— that of a citizen to his or her state. Outside of that relationship, there is no comparable requirement of political justification for coercive acts, even if the actor is a sovereign state. Being one person's mother does not make me a mother to all, and being a sovereign state does not put an actor into a political relationship with all individuals.

We will delay until chapter 4 an in-depth analysis of this argument. For present purposes, only a brief response is necessary. Even if this argument were successful, it would not necessarily support the realist position. For if a state were not acting qua government when it coerced noncitizens, then it would seemingly be acting as a private entity. And unless the realists were to deny that there were ethical limitations on the relationship between private individuals and institutions, there would still be principled limitations. They would be a different set of principles, admittedly, but the difference would not further the realist conclusion. The reason is that the different principles pertinent to the two private actors would be precisely the horizontal ethical principles that realists have sought to avoid. Furthermore, it seems to set their position on its head to explain state power internationally in terms of *lack of sovereign status*, when they have typically justified a state's power in terms of the attributes of *sovereignty*.[30]

Another objection to the vertical thesis is that it neglects the distinctly state-state perspective that many international norms reflect. In many cases a horizontal wrong is also a vertical wrong, but there are some situations in which the wrong cannot be explained fully in vertical terms. At least two sorts of circumstances of this nature come to mind. First, there may be wrongs against a state that do not harm any particular individual from that state. For example, if one state seizes territory over which another is properly sovereign, but which is uninhabited, there may be no individuals that are personally harmed. Perhaps, for instance, one nation has a valid claim to a portion of Antarctica, and another appropriates that territory in order to extract commercially valuable minerals. It is rather strained to treat this as a wrong to the individual citizens of the state whose territory was taken. To the extent that they have been wronged individually, their wrong is only derivative of the injury to their state. If it were not for the existence of their state, the wrong would not be thought to affect them at all.

This example is one that could perhaps with effort be fit into a vertical mold. Under particular political theories, it might be wrong-

[30]This is one of the classic realist arguments. See, for example, Kennan, *American Foreign Policy*, 47–48.

ful to assert sovereignty over some portion of territory even if no individual is affected. The problem is, however, that some political theories might *not* deem such actions wrongful. As to these, the proponent of a purely horizontal approach would state that a vertical analysis is inadequate. It is inadequate, claims the horizontalist, because norms of territorial sovereignty ought not to depend on what some domestic political theory provides. By making such norms contingent on the contours of the relevant domestic political theory, the vertical analysis of international law is incomplete.

A second type of situation in which horizontal analysis is arguably necessary is one in which individuals are injured by a wrongful action, but the nature of the wrongful action cannot be appreciated without reference to the relations between states. Genocide is without a doubt a wrong to an individual; it is murder. However, the crime of genocide cannot be understood without reference to national, religious, or ethnic groupings. Genocide is a different crime from simple murder.[31] It is the deliberate attempted extermination of an identifiable group. To force genocide into the vertical mold is to neglect an important aspect of the crime, namely, that it is directed against a group. For instance, the systematic extermination of a state's nationals is arguably a wrong to the state as well as to the individual victims.

Another example of this sort is failure to honor treaty obligations. Perhaps the best-established principle of international law is the state's obligation to respect its treaties.[32] This obligation cannot really be understood adequately in vertical terms, however. The obligation does not flow to individual citizens but to the other state. A treaty might, for instance, have been signed a hundred years earlier, and none of the original individual beneficiaries is even still alive. This fact would not, however, necessarily affect the validity of the obligation. Again, one might attempt to construe the treaty as an obligation to the current citizens of the nation (so that failure to fulfill

---

[31]See, for example, Hugo Bedau, "Genocide in Vietnam?" and Richard Falk, "Ecocide, Genocide, and the Nuremberg Tradition of Individual Responsibility," in Virginia Held, Sidney Morgenbesser, and Thomas Nagel, eds., *Philosophy, Morality, and International Affairs* (New York: Oxford University Press, 1974).

[32]See Georg Schwarzenberger, *A Manual of International Law* (New York: Praeger, 1967), 151–70.

the obligation is a vertical injury to particular persons) but this interpretation seems rather strained. Their injury seems derivative.

These three examples do not refute the vertical thesis however because the existence of horizontal principles is in no way inconsistent with vertical reasoning. In vertical reasoning, after all, collective entities such as nation states can have rights. In fact, vertical reasoning is directly founded on such collective-entity rights, namely, the rights of states to regulate individuals. Although vertical reasoning does not by itself specify what rights exist between states, it clearly contemplates that nation states are capable of possessing rights. From there, one need merely demonstrate that such rights may include rights and obligations to other states as well. The need for some horizontal norms is not a persuasive objection to vertical analysis.

A third major objection to vertical analysis is that it grants too much power to a state that was founded on an unprincipled domestic political theory. The vertical perspective might seem to increase such a state's power to act internationally because it ties foreign policy to domestic political theory. It might then seem that if a state's domestic theory approved expansionism, it would be entitled to expansionistic acts in international relations. For example, if the Soviet Union were constituted by a theory that required justification of state acts in terms of whether they promoted socialist revolutions, then it would have a basis for invading neighboring countries such as Afghanistan. Similarly, a state that was founded on principles of racial superiority could justify imperialism or even extermination of other peoples.

The difficulty with this objection is that it does not distinguish between a valid political theory and one that is merely held sincerely. It is not enough simply to postulate a political theory; the theory must be convincing. While the formal requirements of the vertical thesis seem to have been met, the dispute over the legitimacy of state acts has merely been shifted to the domestic theory itself. In order for a state to justify its actions, it cannot simply assume a particular political justification. This approach would not be convincing as a matter of domestic political justification, and it would not be convincing as a matter of justifying international actions. Over the centuries, domestic political theorists have not simply taken any offered justification at face value. Standards of normative discourse are as applicable to such hypothesized political justifications in the international context as they are in the domestic context. Although we might for purely intellectual purposes hypothesize implausible theories in order to investigate their consequences, such theorizing is no way adequate to justify particular foreign policies.

A related objection is that the vertical analysis does not offer any way to resolve conflicts between states with fundamentally different political systems. If the system of one state would allow some particular action while the system of the other would not, their constituting political theories cannot (so the argument goes) be used to resolve the conflict. Once again, this argument assumes that the vertical thesis requires a posture of value neutrality. The vertical thesis emphatically does not require a position of ethical relativism, however. It explicitly contemplates that there will be critical evaluations of each nation's political theory, both as a domestic and as an international matter. Admittedly, the vertical thesis does not itself supply the criteria for evaluating political actions. Its metatheoretical imposition of only a formal consistency criterion is, however, a far cry from the position that all political theories are equally valid. Where conflicting political theories are offered, the task is essentially the one facing all domestic political theorists, namely, critical analysis.

What must be conceded is that vertical analysis for this reason explicitly involves international analysts in an undertaking they might otherwise prefer to bypass, namely, assessing the legitimacy of claims that state actors make about domestic political theory. While scholars may not shrink from such a task, institutional decision-making bodies charged with applying international law might be loathe to pass judgment on domestic political philosophies. Thus, it might be said, the vertical thesis provides a theoretically interesting foundation for international normative analysis but a poor support for international legal reasoning that must accommodate, pluralistically, all manner of domestic political theory—right or wrong.

But the example of socialist internationalism illustrates that even in existing international legal decision making, pluralism is only skin deep. To the extent that socialist internationalism (or for that matter, liberal capitalism or Islamic fundamentalism) mandates international aggression, international institutions are not automatically bound to defer to it. An essential element of Marxist (or capitalist or Islamic) thought may be the aggressive promotion of socialism (capitalism or Islam) without regard to national boundaries. To cabin such political philosophies within state borders may seem pluralistic, but the "pluralism" itself passes judgment on essential political claims. Existing international institutions do not really avoid excursions into domestic political philosophy. They simply avoid the appearance of taking controversial political-theoretical positions by not acknowledging the political premises on which they operate.

A final major objection to the vertical thesis is that it is too demanding. The requirements of domestic political theories can never be met in the international setting. The issue is thus whether the vertical thesis is likely to be terribly restrictive—the sort of "moralism" that the realists derided as out of touch with foreign-policy reality. Realists have been concerned not to hamstring our foreign-policy makers' pursuit of the national interest by burdening them with idealistic and overly ambitious goals. The vertical perspective threatens to place serious restrictions on a nation's freedom of action. If it is taken seriously, the realists would fear, it might result in placing important national interests in serious jeopardy. And if applying it seriously would impinge on national interests in this way, it would likely not be of much use to actual policymakers. They would ignore it.

The vertical perspective itself does not dictate how stringent the limitations will be. The stringency of limitations placed by the vertical analysis depends on the stringency of the limitations in the domestic political theory that it projects into the international arena. The realists might fear that a nation that took vertical arguments seriously would be unable to respond adequately to outside threats. But outside threats are not necessarily qualitatively different from inside threats. Both pose severe tests of one's commitment to principle.

Threats from the outside, for instance, are not qualitatively different from threats of revolution, of serious economic breakdown, or of moral and cultural degradation that arise from internal sources. The "war on drugs" may be as threatened by principled limitations as any war with another nation. Internal, as well as external, sources can threaten a society or a way of life. In the United States, for example, civil and political rights commonly have built into them some recognition that in times of serious threat, rights might have to be abridged.[33] Civil libertarians, of course, denounce such doctrines, just as civil disciplinarians think that they are too infrequently invoked. The point here is not to argue that the line should be drawn at one place rather than at another. The point rather is that it is inevitable in both the domestic-policy and the foreign-policy contexts that individual rights and state needs may come in conflict, and this conflict will have to be addressed.

What does, admittedly, seem different in many foreign-policy contexts is the extent of the threat and the difficulty in controlling it. Practically speaking, it is a lot easier to police militant groups that threaten law and order from within than militant groups that operate from without (armed perhaps with long-range weapons or able to retreat to sanctuaries outside the borders). Local groups rarely have the power to overrun or annihilate a state; those that do tend to be in nations that are so weak domestically as to be dubious anyway. It is perhaps too much to ask that American intelligence agencies abide by the fine points of Fourth and Fifth Amendment law when they investigate or interrogate foreign terrorists.

Whatever the difference in the extent and intractability of the threat, however, it is not germane to the problem of whether the same standard should be applied in the domestic and in the international context. If a single standard is applied, it will respond to the relevant differences in situations. That is, if the domestic theory takes into account the state's need on occasion to respond to emergency threats, that need may arise more frequently in the foreign than in the domestic context. But this does not mean that a different set of standards for the two situations is required. A single standard may justify different reactions to different circumstances. A standard of "unreasonable" searches and seizures may permit warrantless wiretapping of terrorist suspects abroad.

In fact, one of the appealing aspects of vertical analysis is that it forces a more open recognition of these less attractive features of domestic political theory. It may be the case that our domestic theories contain exceptions for extreme circumstances even in domestic

---

[33]See, for instance, Schenck v. United States, 249 U.S. 47 (1919), discussed in Laurence Tribe, *American Constitutional Law* (Mineola, N.Y.: Foundation Press, 1978), 608–17.

cases but that we have been able to avoid recognizing them because such circumstances rarely arise domestically. When they do—as in the World War II internment of Japanese Americans—we may be surprised by the ugly and illegitimate sentiments that we find in ourselves with regard to our own citizens and within our own territory. We should not be able to avoid facing these issues simply because they rarely arise in domestic cases and because when they arise internationally, only noncitizens suffer.

Furthermore, as a matter of purely theoretical interest, such attention to domestic theory in cases with international elements can be illuminating. Some assumptions that we make in domestic theory turn out to be incorrect or misleading once we turn to the international arena. For instance, it is widely thought that the basis for political legitimacy is that individuals be allowed to influence the political process through voting. Clearly, this reasoning cannot explain our foreign policy since those affected by our foreign-policy choices are not allowed to vote. Nor does it explain certain cases that seem clearly to be subject to constraints of political legitimacy, such as the treatment of foreigners temporarily visiting the country.

The insistence that political theory applies even to disputes with transnational elements thus raises some provocative challenges to domestic political theory. The next chapter deals with such issues at greater length.

Chapter Three

Boundary Assumptions in Domestic Political Theory

International lawyers might be surprised to hear that some portions of international law should be analyzed according to ordinary domestic political theory. But domestic political theorists would probably be equally surprised. Few have given much thought to the implications of their ideas for the international context, or to the implications of international relations for their ideas. Certainly most of their theories have not been framed with this purpose in mind. Instead, their efforts are directed at the question of domestic political legitimacy. Does a citizen have an obligation to obey his or her own government, and if so, why?[1]

---

[1]Occasionally authors recognize the possibility of noncitizen obligation. In doing so, however, they tend to emphasize the special status that citizen obligations have traditionally been accorded. For example, Robert Paul Wolff states that the anarchist position dismisses as sentimental the special sense of obligation one has toward one's own country: "In a sense, we might characterize the anarchist as a man without a country, for despite the ties which bind him to the land of his childhood, he stands in precisely the same moral relationship to 'his' government as he does to the government of any other country in which he might happen to be staying for a time. When I take a vacation in Great Britain, I obey its laws, both because of prudential self-interest and because of the obvious moral considerations concerning the value of order, the general good consequences of preserving a system of property, and so forth. On my return to the United States, I have a sense of reentering *my* country, and if I think about the matter at all, I imagine myself to stand in a different and more intimate relation to American laws. They have been promulgated by *my* government,

This separation of the two theoretical domains is deeply problematic, however. Political theory and boundary questions cannot be viewed in isolation from one another. Political theorists can no more afford to disregard international boundary issues than international lawyers can afford to disregard traditional political theory. Embedded in the traditional approaches to political theory are boundary assumptions that are crucial to the argument but seldom acknowledged. To have a philosophical theory to account for the phenomenon of political responsibility one must, indeed, have an underlying theory of territorial sovereignty and how it is acquired. But such a theory must be made explicit and defended. This is no easy task; in fact, there are reasons to doubt whether any theory of territorial sovereignty would adequately justify the boundaries of existing nation states and therefore the pattern of political obligations that most theorists seek to explain.

By not addressing boundary issues explicitly, domestic political theorists have simultaneously made things both easier for themselves and harder. Their enterprise is easier because they have taken for granted existing national borders, which play a large part in the legitimacy of a state's coercion of its own citizens. Their enterprise is harder because political theory has committed itself to a particularly difficult phrasing of the question of political justification, namely, why may a state coerce its own citizens? Political theory might instead have asked, why is a state ever entitled to coerce anyone?

As in previous chapters, our argument draws on those parts of the existing literature that recognize a link between political theory and national boundaries. For example, democratic theorists have long seen the importance of identifying the governmental unit within which elections will operate.[2] In addition, two contemporary writers,

---

and I therefore have a special obligation to obey them. But the anarchist tells me that my feeling is purely sentimental and has no objective moral basis'' (*In Defense of Anarchism* [New York: Harper, 1976]). Simmons likewise, in material discussed below, addresses the question of whether one has a special obligation toward one's own government (*Moral Principles and Political Obligations* [Princeton, N.J.: Princeton University Press, 1979], 3–4). The assumption in both cases seems to be that once one has refuted this special obligation, one has undercut much of the traditional learning on political obligation.

[2] See, for instance, Robert Dahl, "Procedural Democracy," in Peter Laslett and James Fishkin, eds., *Philosophy, Politics, and Society* (New Haven, Conn.: Yale University Press, 1979), 108.

John Simmons and Michael Walzer, have addressed in different ways the challenge that boundary issues raise to the process of political justification.[3] Both authors, however, seem to have underestimated how truly difficult boundary issues are for domestic political philosophy. The inability to explain or justify existing national borders does not merely create philosophical difficulties in contexts where the international overtones are apparent. It also undermines any effort to explain coercion in what would seem to be a purely domestic setting.

Political theory attempts to approach political justification as a problem involving only persons: community members having obligations to one another or to a state entity created by or for people. This approach neglects the fact that governmental coercion is mediated by reference to *land*. Until one justifies the special relationship of sovereignty that a nation has to its territory, it is not possible either to identify which individuals are subject to state coercion or to justify coercion over the individuals who *are* bound.

The Importance of Boundaries

A few examples, hypothetical and real, will illustrate how crucial boundary issues are to the problem of political obligation. Assume that state coercion is thought to be justifiable in terms of the state's democratic electoral procedures. A citizen has political obligations, so this theory goes, because he or she is entitled to vote in the elections that choose officials and express public-policy preferences. If the right to vote justifies coercion, then all those entitled to vote (or, perhaps, all those entitled to vote when they reach the age of majority, and have not committed felonies, and so forth) are obligated to obey.

But what if the state wishes to annex a neighboring country? Can it merely extend to all of that country's inhabitants the right to vote in the first state's local elections? Under the simple "right to vote implies obligation to obey" formula, the citizens of the neighboring state would then have an obligation to support the first one. But this

[3]Michael Walzer, *Spheres of Justice* (New York: Basic Books, 1983); Simmons, *Moral Principles*.

seems most implausible. More specifically, what if the United States were unilaterally to extend to the leaders of the Soviet Union the right to vote in U.S. elections? Surely this would not oblige them to obey U.S. law. It seems that it is only within some specific group of persons (citizens, maybe?) that a democracy can grant the right to vote and expect obedience in exchange. There must be some sort of boundary rule. But this group is not itself defined in terms of the right to vote.

The same point can be made about any effort to found political obligations on the granting of substantive (as opposed to participatory) rights. To establish an obligation to obey, a government would only have to extend the substantive rights in question. For example, a liberal might seek to justify political authority on the grounds that a state respects privacy, promotes free speech, guarantees religious freedom, and so forth. But the state may not simply guarantee these rights to persons from the world at large and then claim the right to coerce them. The liberal's argument, in other words, assumes a group of citizens to which it applies. It needs an answer to the boundary problem.

While these hypothetical problems may seem fanciful, actual practical problems can arise. An example from the American experience is the Civil War. The difference between the northerner and the southerner was not so much a disagreement about the necessity for democratic processes (although, of course, there were different views about slavery and about centralized power). The disagreement was more over the appropriate unit within which democracy was supposed to operate. It was not over whether voting creates an obligation to obey; southerners would have been perfectly happy to give up the right to vote in federal elections in exchange for peaceful seccession. The question was whether they could legitimately be compelled to accept the exchange of the right to vote for the obligation to obey. Within what boundary should this forced exchange be operative?

As this example suggests, the boundary issue assumes peculiarly critical importance between two states that are structurally equivalent with regard to the substantive and procedural aspects of political theory—states, that is, that are different instantiations of the same justifying theory. Where the constituting political theories of two states respect the same substantive and procedural rights, the reason for owing allegiance to one state rather than to the other cannot be explained in substantive or procedural terms. It must turn on the answer to the boundary question.

Boundary questions are as crucial to domestic theory as they are to international law, although they are framed in different ways. I argued in the last chapter that international law requires a comparison between two vertical relationships, namely, that between a state and a person over whom authority exists and that between a state and a person over whom authority does not exist. It is possible to view the same comparison from another perspective. Instead of asking about a state's proper stance toward two different individuals, one within its authority and one possibly not, one can make a comparison between an individual's proper attitude toward two different states, with authority owing to one but possibly not to the other (see Figure 3).

Again, the comparison is between two vertical relations, and one is a secure relationship of authority and one is open to doubt. But stating the comparison in this manner makes the relevance of the issue to domestic political theory more apparent. The question now becomes, to which state (or states) does an individual owe political obligations? What is it about an individual's relationship with one particular state that is special and creates duties or obligations, when his or her relationship with other states creates no such duties or obligations?

Any political justification must be able to answer this question. If the criteria of political legitimacy are adequately stated, they should differentiate one's relationship with a state possessing legitimate authority from one's relationship with a state lacking legitimate authority. A justification is not adequate if it cannot differentiate be-

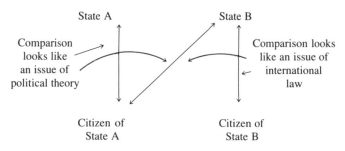

Figure 3. Diagonal relations in domestic and international theory

tween states to which one owes an obligation and those to which one does not. As we have suggested, however, the differentiation cannot always be made on the basis of the substantive justice or the procedural fairness of the two states; two states may be equally fair and just. In these cases, some boundary criterion is necessary to explain why obligations are owing to one state but not to the other.

Particularized Obligations

The author that has addressed the relevance of boundary issues to domestic political justification at greatest length and in greatest depth is A. J. Simmons.[4] Simmons asks, why does an individual have a special obligation to obey his or her own government as opposed to the government of the state in which he or she is temporarily present or resident? He calls this issue the problem of particularization.

His phrasing of the question reflects the traditional assumption that the key boundary element is citizenship. Simmons examines several of the traditionally offered examples of political justification and finds them all wanting, concluding that one has no greater obligation toward one's own state than toward the state in which one is present. His interest is not with boundary problems per se but with the problem of domestic justification. His argument that there are no philosophically defensible particularized obligations is designed to show that one has no particular obligation to obey or support one's own government.

Of special interest here is his discussion of political responsibilities founded on the natural duty of justice.[5] This theory of political responsibility, which he ascribes to John Rawls, states that citizens have a duty to support all just institutions that apply to them.[6] The phrase "that apply to them" is the crucial one. Rawls does not explain the phrase, but some qualification of the duty to support just institutions is clearly necessary. It would go too far to suggest that individuals have equal responsibilities to support all just institutions

[4]Simmons, *Moral Principles*.
[5]Simmons, *Moral Principles*, chap. 6, especially pp. 147–52.
[6]John Rawls, *A Theory of Justice* (Cambridge, Mass.: Harvard University Press, 1971), 334.

whatsoever. Simmons's point is basically the same point that I made earlier in the argument that a political justification must have a boundary criterion. Neither procedural fairness nor substantive justice alone is an adequate justification, because neither differentiates individuals with an obligation from those with no obligation. The qualification that the just institution must "apply" to you is just such a boundary criterion.

But narrowing the institutions to only those that "apply" to you is not easy. Simmons uses the example of a society, established in one geographical area for the advancement of philosophy, that collects dues and engages in good deeds.[7] It would not seem appropriate to say that the society and its rules "apply" to all philosophers, he says, even though philosophers everywhere might benefit from it. To allow the founders this right to define the range of applicability would give them the unilateral opportunity to create duties in others.

Nor, says Simmons, should application simply be defined in geographical terms. For instance, he next hypothesizes that a reservation of philosophers is operated and controlled by this society. If children are born on the reservation, and grow to maturity there, does the institution apply in the Rawlsian sense in such a way as to create a duty to obey? Simmons believes that one cannot have a political responsibility thrust on one in this way. An institution can only come to apply to you in the pertinent sense by your voluntarily undertaking a relationship with it.

But then, he says, the supposed explanation based on a natural duty toward just institutions degenerates into a more usual explanation based on voluntaristic assumption of obligations, the sort of explanation that he undermines elsewhere in his book. He argues that although voluntarist explanations are possibly adequate in theory, as a matter of empirical fact, they would not bind a high percentage of a state's citizens, for few citizens have engaged in the sort of deliberate actions that amount to voluntary assumption of political responsibilities.

Simmons is certainly correct in raising the following basic problem. Either the obligation to obey the government is based on some quality that the government has, such as substantive justice, or it is

[7]Simmons, *Moral Principles*, 148–50.

based on some relationship that it has with particular people. It cannot be based merely on a characteristic of the government because such a basis would fail to differentiate between those persons (presumably citizens) who are bound and those who are not. The government either has or does not have these qualities, and so either everyone is bound or no one is. Therefore, in order to be adequately particularized, the obligation to support a government must be founded on a relationship between the individual and the state, rather than on just the character of the state.

While Simmons is correct about the need for particularization, his insistence on voluntariness in the state-individual relationship is not quite right. This insistence, moreover, obscures the magnitude of the problem that his arguments uncover. It is not clear that the missing link is the one that Simmons supposes, namely, voluntary association with one nation or another. Given his own purposes, it is enough to show that the natural duty of justice really boils down to a theory of voluntary assumption of obligations. Simmons seeks to undercut traditional theory. Reduction of the natural duty to support just institutions to a voluntaristic approach is sufficiently undercutting for his purposes because it describes actual state-individual relationships in only a very few cases.

But voluntary assumption is not a sufficient condition for the legitimacy of coercion as he seems to argue. To the contrary, even an assumption that is voluntary according to Simmons's own criteria is very likely to provide inadequate justification. This is shown in two examples he cites. He apparently believes that they evince sufficient voluntary activity to justify political responsibilities; both are fallacious in this regard. Each represents a modification of a theory of justification offered by someone else, and Simmons suggests that with the modification the justification is theoretically adequate in each, though it fails to include many people. But in showing how these voluntarist solutions are not even adequate as a theoretical matter, we will see that the boundary problems Simmons describes are too serious to be solved merely by incorporating a requirement of voluntary affiliation. Simmons argues that since voluntariness is a necessary condition, very few people are legitimately obligated. What he fails to observe is that, absent a prior showing of territorial sovereignty, voluntariness itself is not sufficient.

The Importance of Territorial Sovereignty

TACIT CONSENT

The first of Simmons's two examples represents justification based on tacit consent. Tacit consent is an appealing potential justification. Given the attractions of basing political responsibilities on a citizen's consent, but conceding the obvious embarrassment that most citizens have not explicitly consented, the next best alternative might be a theory that citizens had implicitly or tacitly agreed to support their governments. Locke, for instance, relied on tacit consent when he argued that by residing or remaining in a country, or even perhaps by using its highways, an individual assumed an obligation to obey.[8]

This fiction is no more satisfying to Simmons than it has been to others who have considered it.[9] He does, however, attempt to rehabilitate the theory by describing certain circumstances in which an argument of tacit consent might be convincing. For instance, as a "genuine instance of tacit consent" he offers the following:

> Chairman Jones stands at the close of the company's board meeting and announces, "There will be a meeting of the board at which attendance will be mandatory next Tuesday at 8:00, rather than at our usual Thursday time. Any objections?" The board members remain silent. In remaining silent and inactive, they have all tacitly consented to the chairman's proposal to make a schedule change (assuming, of course, that none of the members is asleep, or failed to hear, etc.). As a result, they have given the chairman the right (which he does not normally have) to reschedule the meeting, and they have undertaken the obligation to attend at the new time.[10]

But such genuine instances of tacit consent, Simmons argues, are not common in political life. Therefore, the tacit-consent theory is saved in principle only to become irrelevant in fact.

---

[8]John Locke, *Second Treatise of Government*, sec. 119.
[9]See, for example, Hanna Pitkin, "Obligation and Consent-I," *American Political Science Review* 59 (December 1965), 995; David Hume, "Of the Original Contract," in Alisdair MacIntyre, ed., *Hume's Ethical Writings* (New York: Collier Books, 1965), 263.
[10]Simmons, *Moral Principles*, 79–80.

Now what are the characteristics of this example that make an imputation of tacit consent seem reasonable? Simmons lists five.[11] The individuals must be aware of the situation and that consent is being requested; there must be a reasonable period of time for expression of dissent; it must be clear by what point the objection must have been made; it must be reasonably easy to express consent; and the consequences of dissent must not penalize or deter such expressions. For example, there would be no tacit consent if the members had to express dissent by chopping off their right arm at the elbow.

Whether or not these conditions are *necessary* for a finding of tacit consent, however, they are not (despite Simmons's suggestion) really *sufficient*. What if we were to change the example in only one way: the announcement is made not by the chairman of the board but by a window washer who calls into the room from a platform hanging outside the window. Here, as in Simmons's example, the five conditions are all met. But it seems that the members of the board would be entitled to ignore the window washer, because as the board members are well aware, the window washer has no authority to propose schedule changes for board meetings. Simmons's example, in other words, hinges in part on the fact that the chairman has already been acknowledged to have some kind of authority to propose schedule changes; yet it is precisely this authority that the tacit consent theory is supposed to explain.

The example is admittedly unrealistic, because it is hard to imagine a window washer doing such a thing. One would be unlikely to announce a change in meeting time if one had no legitimate involvement with, or authority over, the issue. This aspect only serves to highlight the general point, however. The chairman has authority to propose a schedule change because of a general background of legitimate authority over such issues. If a member of the board were to make the suggestion, it would be less plausible, although somewhat arguable, for the motion to carry simply because no one opposed it. The less the authority of the person making the proposal, the less plausible the argument from tacit consent.

A more illuminating example of the problem with Simmons's

[11]Simmons, *Moral Principles*, 80–81.

criteria can be found in a situation closer to home. Locke's explanation of state authority in terms of tacit consent expressed by residing
or being present in a state would work under Simmons's analysis so
long as the citizens were aware of the request for consent, it was easy
enough to dissent, and so forth. Of course, these criteria are not all
true in fact. This is Simmons's point. But, more relevant for present
purposes, even if all of these conditions were met, they would not be
sufficient unless it were assumed that the state had some kind of
authority over the territory itself.

For example, the United States could not base tacit consent to U.S.
authority on a person's residing in Canada, regardless of whether it
notified everyone of its intent to do so and it was easy for people to
leave Canada and so forth. Residing in Canada can at most signify
tacit consent to Canadian authority, not to U.S. authority, even
though the situations in the two countries are probably equal with
regard to Simmons's five criteria—the U.S. government could give
just as much notice, objecting to Canadian law by leaving Canada is
just as convenient as objecting to American law by leaving Canada,
and so forth. His five criteria do not differentiate on the grounds of
which state is proposing that remaining in Canada constitutes consent
to its own laws, although the identity of the state is obviously important.

Locke's example, similarly, takes for granted that England has
authority over the territory of England. It is only because of this
authority that it makes sense to suggest that by residing in England
one consents to the authority of England. Contrast the situation, for
example, in which a French king claimed a right to rule some portion
of England, perhaps according to some doubtful historical claim.
Pursuant to this claim, the French king states that all those present in
that territory tacitly consent to his authority by remaining there. The
English citizens would be entirely entitled to dispute this assertion—
or to ignore it. They would deny the obligation on the ground that the
French king has no authority within the territory and therefore no
right to attach conditions to a subject's remaining within it. Only if
the French king's sovereignty over the territory came to be recognized would the argument be convincing. Tacit consent, therefore,
assumes the very political authority it seeks to establish. It turns on
prior assumptions about sovereignty.

ACCEPTANCE OF BENEFITS

A second theory that Simmons discusses and tries to rehabilitate, namely, the acceptance of benefits, likewise turns on such assumptions. It has been argued that when an institution creates benefits through the voluntary cooperation of its members, those who share in the benefits have an obligation to support the institution through their cooperation.[12] Simmons is doubtful about this argument, in large part because one might receive benefits from the cooperation of others without having solicited the benefit in any way.[13] In this respect, his view is somewhat similar to that of Robert Nozick, although Simmons points to important differences.[14]

In differentiating between benefits that create political obligations and those that do not, Simmons argues that in some cases benefits are "accepted" and in others they are merely "received." Only the former is an adequate basis for political obligation. Accepting a benefit, he says, involves either trying to get (and succeeding in getting) the benefit or taking the benefit willingly and knowingly.[15] As in his treatment of the tacit-consent argument, and also of the natural-duty-of-justice argument, he seeks to rehabilitate an overly broad justification by incorporating a requirement that the political responsibility be based on some voluntary action.

But as we have suggested with regard to these arguments, a voluntaristic requirement, on closer examination, can be shown not to cure the problems. The paradigm example in which acceptance of benefits is thought to provide a political justification is the situation where a group of individuals band together and make sacrifices in order to produce some commonly valued commodity. Intuition suggests that free riders—those who have refused to make sacrifices—are not entitled to share in the benefits. If they do so, according to the argument, they have implicitly undertaken to abide by the rules of the group that dictates what sacrifices must be made. Thus if a citizen

---

[12]He discusses the versions of this theory put forth by Hart and Rawls. John Rawls, "Legal Obligation and the Duty of Fair Play," in Sidney Hook, ed., *Law and Philosophy* (New York: New York University Press, 1964); Herbert Hart, "Are There Any Natural Rights?" *Philosophical Review* 64 (April 1955).

[13]Simmons, *Moral Principles*, 107–8.

[14]Simmons, *Moral Principles*, 118–36.

[15]Simmons, *Moral Principles*, 138–39.

drinks from a common well that was constructed by a group of other citizens, the citizen assumes a responsibility to help pay for and maintain the well.[16]

Again, however, this argument turns on a prior assumption that authority exists. An essential element of such examples is the intuition that the group members are entitled to what they have created. If they had no entitlement to the well or its water, then the appropriator of benefits would not be appropriating anything of theirs even if he or she went out of his or her way to "accept" benefits, to use Simmons's terminology. For example, if the well diggers had illegitimately dug a well on the free rider's property, then the mere fact that their efforts made the benefit available would probably not allow them to place conditions on his use of his own water.

This point is clearer in the international context. Assume that the United States is full of diligent and talented individuals who make many sacrifices to build their country into a wealthy and powerful one; they pay taxes, they abide by the laws, they refrain from destructive behavior, and so forth. The result is that Americans become very prosperous and many Canadian industries spring up along the border to take advantage of the benefits of dealing with American tourists who drive across the border to spend the wealth that they have accumulated by their industrious behavior. Surely, even though a Canadian who relocates to such a border town has both tried to get the benefit of the Americans' increased wealth and has taken it willingly and knowingly, the United States does not have an adequate basis for compelling the Canadian to comply with American insitutions that require the industrious behavior.[17] Admittedly, if a Canadian relocated in the United States in order to receive the benefit of doing business with Americans, one might see a basis for requiring compliance with American law. And the explanation might be phrased in

[16]This is Simmons's example, in which he seems to believe that obligations exist (*Moral Principles*, 127).

[17]Simmons would apparently agree: "We cannot accept an account of political obligation which binds noncitizens to do their part in a foreign country's cooperative political enterprises" (*Moral Principles*, 137). See also Kent Greenawalt's example in *Conflicts of Law and Morality* (New York: Oxford University Press, 1987), 126: "If the workers of a foreign country accept lower wages to produce cars at a lower price, and I am able to purchase for $8,000 a car for which I would have been willing to pay $9,000, I owe no duty of fair play to the workers."

terms of "receiving the benefits of American law." But there seems to be a world of difference between receiving them in the United States and receiving them in Canada.

Tacit-consent and acceptance-of-benefits arguments both turn, therefore, on implicit assumptions about the boundaries of sovereignty. An individual who tacitly consents, or who accepts benefits, within the territory is in a different position from one who does so while remaining outside. A final example, express consent, will illustrate the extent to which political theories contain within them such hidden boundary assumptions. Express consent has generally been thought to provide a strong theoretical foundation for political obligation, although it is not often satisfied in practice because of its strictness.

Furthermore, it would seem to be the theory that most nearly provides a satisfactory answer to the boundary issue. Which governments is one obligated to obey? Exactly those to which explicit consent has been given. Unlike the duty to support just governments, explicit consent allows an individual to differentiate among the existing governments so that there is no indiscriminate obligation to obey all of them. Explicit consent is relational, whereas substantive justice is a quality that the government either possesses or does not possess and that does not differentiate between persons.

But explicit-consent theory is prone to the same sovereignty-based difficulties that plagued the other approaches. Take what might be considered the strongest example of express consent: an immigrant arriving in the United States is required, as a condition of admission, to agree to obey the laws of the United States and to support its government. This is a clearer example than one usually finds, because with regard to lifelong inhabitants, there is rarely a specific occasion that can be pointed to as the moment of consent. Of course, one might be concerned about the voluntariness of the consent if the immigrant were an asylum seeker who was desparate to gain admission, but let us assume that in the case in question the would-be immigrant is under no particular danger at home, and therefore under no duress.

Still, the example depends on the fact that U.S. immigration officials have a right to keep the would-be immigrant out of the country. Contrast the example with a flotilla from the Canadian navy that stops ships off the North American coast, refusing to allow passage to the United States unless the passengers agree to obey Canadian law after they have landed in the United States. Even if the immigrant expressly consents to these conditions as a price of entry to the United States, such consent would not count as the basis for a continuing obligation to obey. The consent given to American immigration officials, if it counts as a basis of obligation, counts only because as officials of the sovereign that is entitled to exercise authority within the United States, they are entitled to impose conditions in ways that officials of another country would not be.

Territory-specific Boundary Criteria

These arguments all have the same logical form. The proposed political theory says that the basis for political obligation is x (accepting benefits, residing in the country, entering the country, or something of that sort). The voluntarism argument requires that x be something that can be either done or not done without such great cost that the choice no longer is a free choice and that the consequences of chosing to do x be reasonably clear in advance. None of this addresses, however, the question of why the sovereign is entitled to conclude that doing x amounts to assuming an obligation to obey.

There are two ways in which such a conclusion might be reached. First, if the sovereign is entitled to regulate the doing of x, it is entitled to impose costs on doing x, such as a requirement of obedience to the law. For example, if the state is entitled to impose conditions on residing in the country, then it may require all those who live in the country to obey the law. The very imposition of such a rule, however, requires that sovereignty already exist. The sovereign is only entitled to impose costs based on the doing of x when it is entitled to regulate x in the first place. This basis for predicating obligation on the doing of x therefore cannot explain the right to rule because it depends on prior sovereignty.[18]

---

[18]The sole possible exception seems to be express consent where nothing is received in exchange. Whenever the individual receives something in exchange for the promise, however, there are problems concerning why the state would have had a right to withhold that quid pro quo.

A second possible interpretation of the argument seems at first to avoid this circularity. The sovereign is not imposing a cost on doing x but instead is *making an inference* from x. It does not take political authority to make an inference; philosophers, for instance, propose rules about what constitutes consent without having any sovereign authority, merely from the belief that the arguments are normatively convincing. There is a difference, for example, between saying "eating cornflakes for breakfast shall henceforth count as consent to the U.S. government" and saying "explicitly promising to obey the U.S. government of your own free will shall count as consent." The latter seems a plausible inference; it is supported by reason rather than authority.

The former might perhaps be adopted as a convention, in which case it might be fair to impose political obligations on the basis of eating cornflakes. But such a convention must be authoritative to be effective, because it treats some arbitrary action as a signal for a meaning that the action would not otherwise have. Making an explicit promise, in contrast, does not (so the argument would go) derive its ability to justify coercion from an arbitrary convention that must be authoritatively established. It is an inference that even an observer acting without political authority, such as a philosopher, might make. It is reasonable to infer that a person who says "I promise to obey the U.S. government" is actually, thereafter, obligated to obey the U.S. government.

Even if there are inferences of this sort, which do not rely on authoritative convention, this possibility offers little support for an effort to build political theory without boundary conditions. Any action that even arguably supports an intuitive (nonconventional) inference of assuming political obligation must be an action taken somehow with reference to the existing boundaries of the state. It must, somehow, be territory specific. When philosophers assert such theories, for instance, they respect the sovereign outlines of existing states. The action must be taken with reference to the state to which one owes an obligation, for how could doing x single out one state from the others? Residing in England is intuitively plausible as a sign of assent only to the government of England, not of China. Promising to obey the government of the United States assumes a particular territorial United States and an entity that governs it.

But by particularizing the activity x so that it makes reference to only one state (residing in state A, entering into state A, being born in state A, accepting benefits in state A, or something similar), one presupposes that the government of the state has a special relationship with the territory of the state such that it is intuitively natural to infer political obligations based on activities happening there. That is, one is presupposing sovereign boundaries.

The unavoidable fact is that we assume states to have geographical limitations; they do not possess authority to regulate the entire world. Any description of x that is not territory-specific violates intuitions that the territorial scope of nation states is limited.[19] Yet, sovereignty is presupposed when the description of x is made territory specific. As soon as one specifies a particular geographical description to limit activity x as a sufficient condition for an obligation to obey, one has made an assumption that the state is sovereign over that territory—a normative assumption that is prior to the theory that says x is an adequate foundation for political obligation.

The boundary theory that delineates the territorial sovereignty of a state is therefore an important element of all political theories that have been offered to justify state coercion. Boundary theories lurk implicitly in the background, as where Locke says that residing *in the state* or being present *in the state* is an adequate basis for an obligation to obey the state. Obviously, there has to be a state—with a defined territory—before such claims can be made. The jurisdictional boundaries, the limits within which domestic political theories operate, are as important to the obligation to obey as the domestic political theories themselves. By what right did England come to exercise sovereignty over a piece of territory so that it may claim that persons who engage in certain activities there are subject to its legitimate exercise of power? No theory of domestic political justification is possible without an answer to such questions.

---

[19]Perhaps one might gratuitously promise to obey the U.S. government: If nothing is received in exchange and the enforceability of the promise was not thought to depend on where it was made, then it might be binding even if not territory specific. This sort of obligation more nearly resembles the duties one assumes on entering an institution like the Catholic church, which is not territorially limited. It seems an implausible basis for political obligations to nation states.

The Problem of the Status Quo

A major difficulty with formulating an answer to such questions is that the answer would have to justify the national boundaries that currently exist in order to explain why one has obligations to the nation in which one is present or of which one is currently a citizen. The boundary assumptions on which political obligations are implicitly founded are the international status quo.

The close relationship between political justification and the status quo can be illustrated by some arguments made by Michael Walzer.[20] In *Spheres of Justice*, Walzer does not deal directly with the problem of political justification that we are addressing, namely, does one have an obligation to obey one's state? His analysis of membership focuses on immigration, not political coercion generally. However, much that he says is relevant to the question of justification as we have been framing it, and moreover, he is one of the few authors who deal directly with the sort of boundary issues that we have been discussing.

Walzer is concerned with the distribution of membership in a society. How may a society make decisions about whom it should admit? Given that other social goods are distributed on the basis of who is a member, the question of whom to admit is crucial to the distribution of everything else. Walzer believes that societies have a considerable degree of freedom to preserve their distinctive characters by selective admissions.[21] This freedom is not absolute: for instance, a state may have obligations to admit refugees in some circumstances,[22] and if it has more territory than it needs, it may have responsibilities to admit those in dire need.[23] However, because a state is an expression of communal identity, it cannot be forced to become completely open to anyone that would wish to immigrate.

As Walzer recognizes, this theory of group identity is intimately linked to dominion over territory. It might seem possible, otherwise,

[20]Walzer, *Spheres of Justice*. In what follows I owe a debt to a paper written by Tim Macht and a number of conversations with him.
[21]Walzer, *Spheres of Justice*, chap. 2.
[22]Walzer, *Spheres of Justice*, 61–62.
[23]Walzer, *Spheres of Justice*, 51.

to construct a theory of group identity that does not depend on prior assumptions about territorial sovereignty. One might say that autonomous individuals have a right to express themselves by joining groups, and it would violate their autonomy to force them to admit unwanted strangers to their groups.[24] In this simple form, this argument is about membership, but it is less plausible than the more complex argument that Walzer actually makes. In its simple form, the group-identity argument explains why it would violate autonomy to force the group to admit unwanted strangers. But what it does not do is to explain why the group should be able to exclude unwanted strangers from living on a particular piece of land. After all, the members of the group could maintain their exclusive "club," to use Walzer's analogy, even if there were strangers living in their territorial midst.

Something more than this simple autonomy argument must therefore be offered in order to explain why the group can maintain its identity *by excluding people geographically.* Just as there must be a theory of territorial sovereignty underlying any argument about express or tacit consent or receipt of benefits so there must be a theory of territorial sovereignty that explains why a group may maintain its identity through excluding outsiders geographically. One virtue of Walzer's argument is that he clearly recognizes that what is at stake is not simply the homogeneity of membership in an organization but also homogeneity of residence within a particular geographical area.[25] Walzer deals with this question in the following way:

> Nations look for [territorial status] because . . . the link between people and land is a crucial feature of national identity. Their leaders understand, moreover, that because so many critical issues (including issues of distributive justices, such as welfare, education, and so on) can best be resolved within geographical units, the focus of political life can never be established elsewhere. . . . That's why borders, and the movements of individuals and groups across borders, are bitterly disputed as soon as imperial rule recedes and nations begin the process of "liberation." . . . Hence the theory of justice must allow for the

---

[24]Compare the argument by Peter Schuck and Rogers Smith in *Citizenship without Consent: Illegal Aliens in the American Polity* (New Haven, Conn.: Yale University Press, 1985).

[25]Walzer, *Spheres of Justice,* 46.

> territorial state, specifying the rights of its inhabitants and recognizing
> the collective right of admission and refusal. (P. 44)

Territorial sovereignty is justified, in other words, because it is important to the expression of group identity. For all practical purposes, societies must be organized territorially, and this is the source of the right to exclude.

What is important for present purposes is the extent to which this argument rationalizes the status quo. Consider hypothetically a new social movement that emphasizes values that are not the norm in any existing society, a combination, perhaps, of communal ownership of property with group marriage. Assume that the adherents to this social movement are not at present persecuted for their beliefs, but they do not have the social support for their way of life that they would like. They are geographically dispersed, and they would like to form an exclusive territorial community where their children would be brought up to respect their communalism as the highest way of life. All too frequently, as it is, their children are diverted by the materialistic individualism that pervades existing cultures.

Walzer's theory does not allow them any way to achieve territorial self-expression. Any nation can exclude them on the basis of distaste for their culture, if it threatens the social beliefs of the current citizens. Walzer would not force any nation to admit them over such cultural objections, because they are not in physical danger, have not been abused, and are not necessitous. Even if they could gain admission, they would not be able to remove existing residents to achieve homogeneity. The right of existing communities to self-expression through territorial homogeneity therefore trumps any claim by this new group to territorial homogeneity. The status quo prevails.

Now, there may be good reasons to preserve the status quo. The practical costs of shifting populations around are enormous. As Walzer recognizes, people develop expectations about, and affections for, the places where they live.[26] Besides, once the new group was ensconced, it might have to give way in turn to still another group that wanted a chance to further its own group identity through territorial self-expression. The point is not that Walzer ought to require existing

[26]Walzer, *Spheres of Justice*, 44.

states to hand over some or all of their territory but that in a choice between two groups that have equal claims to territorial self-expression, the choice is made on the basis of who got there first.

More than anyone else, perhaps, Walzer recognizes the importance of territorial boundaries to political theory. At bottom, however, even his more territorially sophisticated arguments require a presumption in favor of the territorial status quo. Like the theories of political justification that we investigated earlier, his theory takes for granted the current distribution of territory into nation states, except in extreme circumstances. For purposes either of justifying immigration controls or of justifying political coercion generally, the territorial status quo is an essential foundational element.

Immigration restrictions and legislation are linked in that both are ways of enforcing social norms, one by restrictive admission and the other by coercion of those already present. In both, whoever acquires authority first can leverage territorial sovereignty into political power in a way that later groups cannot. If arguments about express consent, tacit consent, and so forth depend on prior assumptions of territorial sovereignty, the assumptions are necessarily about existing territorial states. In a similar vein, our hypothetical communal group cannot make arguments of tacit or express consent to ground a claim to legislate in support of their chosen life-style, because they are not already in possession of some plot of land. Groups that possess territory have wide latitude to legislate their life-style by extracting consent to this life-style as a condition for entry or naturalization. Unless enough communalists were admitted to shift the local balance of power (and Walzer says that a state need not admit so many), the early settlers can impose their legislative choices on new settlers, as well as limit the number of new settlers.

Why is this a problem? After all, as just noted, there are good practical reasons for favoring the status quo. It should be clear, however, that these good practical reasons do not really offer much consolation to the group that either is completely excluded or is required to support the existing government as a condition of admission. Whether the context is immigration policy or political justification, the burdened group is not really offered an explanation of why it deserves the treatment that it gets. The communal group that we hypothesized seems no less deserving than existing groups that have their own states. It is just that, practically speaking, there is no way to give all groups what they want because the land surface of the globe is limited. And if they are admitted on condition that they support the existing state, the fact that there are practical reasons to prefer existing states does not show that they are not as deserving of a government of their own as are the earlier settlers.

A second reason makes this preference for the status quo even more problematic with regard to political justification. Because the identity of the state to which one owes obligations is a function of existing national boundaries, one's political obligations are determined by the vagaries of the historical process that generated these boundaries. As we know, there was never any central distribution of territory based on any normatively defensible scheme. Instead, existing boundaries are the product of centuries of warfare, imperialism and subsequent liberation, and every other variety of naked power politics. This is a problem because the question of political obligation has been needlessly posed in the most particularized way, namely, in terms of the relationship between a state and its citizens.

Justifying Particular Relationships

Political justification is typically discussed in terms of whether one has an obligation to one's own state. The question is not just about a type of relationship in the abstract but about a particular pattern of relationships between each human being and his or her country of residence. What the question signifies, and why it need not be posed in this way, can be appreciated by comparing it with the way we talk about the institution of private property.

Justifying property ownership can be separated into two different issues, the general concept of private property and the specific distribution of private property that currently exists. Most justifications address the former. To justify the institution of private property, one would not have to show that Brilmayer is entitled to the Dutch colonial house at 200 Clark Avenue, which according to the land records belongs to her, nor to the Baldwin grand piano that sits in her parlor. One can consider the institution generally, without addressing the present distribution.

Similarly, one might discuss the morality of slavery in general in terms of whether it is proper for one human being to own another. One can conclude that slavery would be immoral without ever addressing an existing pattern of slave holdings. Or a southerner before the Civil War could have coherently believed that slavery was generally permissible in the abstract but that the existing distribution of slaves was unfair (because, for instance, poor white people should own as many slaves as rich white people). Whether Smith is really entitled to the particular slaves that she "legally owns" is therefore not the same question as whether ownership of another person, as a general matter, is justifiable. With regard to ownership of labor, one can ask whether it is possible to own labor—a general question—or one can ask, for example: Does one own one's own labor? Does one own one's children's labor? Does one own the labor of the person to whom one pays a salary?

In this respect, property ownership is the same as territorial sovereignty; both are, after all, ways that human beings and their legal and political institutions relate to concrete *things*. There are, therefore, two different ways to approach political justification. First, one might address the general problem independent of any particular examples of it. One might ask, is it ever possible to owe an obligation to support a government? This is the way in which Robert Paul Wolff at times addresses the issue in *In Defense of Anarchism*.[27] He speaks generally about the autonomy of an individual and points out that obedience sometimes means subordinating one's own beliefs about what is right to the commands of an authority. The more common phrasing concerns the particular distribution of political authority that currently exists. Does one have an obligation to support one's own government (or, sometimes, the government of the territory in which one is present)? The question is like asking whether one owns one's own labor (or the labor of one's employee). Such issues are the particularized obligations of which Simmons writes.

Justification of these specific relationships must show not only that political obligations are possible but also that the particular citizen-state relationships that currently exist give rise to obligations. Even assuming that the first can be shown, there is no guarantee that the

[27]Wolff, *In Defense of Anarchism*, chap. 1.

second can also be shown. There is virtually no reason to equate the general and the specific questions.[28] It is possible that the general institution of political obligation is perfectly defensible but no one has any obligation to the state of which he or she is currently a citizen. Indeed, when Simmons argues that consent is a good theory but one rarely satisfied in practice, his argument is essentially that the general question can be answered but the specific one cannot.

Unlike political theorists, property theorists by and large do not seem to feel the need to focus on the harder of the two questions, namely, the justification of the prevailing distribution of property. By choosing the more difficult issue, they would deal themselves a problem that seems virtually insoluble. It is such a seemingly insoluble phrasing of the problem that the political theorists have chosen to address.

The Problem of Arbitrary Distribution

This is the point in the argument at which it becomes crucial that the existing pattern of state-citizen relationship is not the product of any normatively defensible distribution. Given that the existing distribution of territory is almost entirely a product of power politics and that all theories of political obligation depend on the existing distribution, it would be a truly unaccountable coincidence if our existing pattern of political relationships happened to be fair. It is as though we set out to justify a distribution of property that was the result of the strongest, meanest, and smartest individuals grabbing everything they could ruthlessly. If, as seems likely, there is nothing to be said in favor of such a process of distribution, then it seems highly unlikely that the resulting distribution will be justifiable.[29]

With regard to private property, arguments can be made about a

[28]To some degree, it should be conceded, one's idea of what the institution of private property *is* is shaped by existing the distributions that we see around us. The general concept is dependent on specific examples, so that the two are not totally independent.

[29]One such theory might be based on the analysis of the moral force of the status quo contained in Russell Hardin, "Does Might Make Right?" in J. Roland Pennock and John Chapman, eds., *Nomos* 29, *Authority Revisited* (New York: New York University Press, 1987).

fair process of exchange that supply some element of justification for
the existing distribution. One might claim that, given the legal sanc-
tions against theft and in favor of contract, the transfers of property
that have occurred over the last few centuries have resulted in a fair
allocation. Respect for the status quo would then be defensible. Of
course, this is a highly controversial argument, and my point is,
emphatically, not to press it. My point is merely that even if such an
argument were thought convincing, no comparable argument could
be made with regard to territorial sovereignty.

If one believed that there were rules of international law and that
existing territorial allocation reflected only transfer in accordance
with those rules, then there might be a moral justification for the
pattern of state-citizen relationships that we currently see. However,
the fact that I am a citizen of the United States and not of Great Britain
is a product of the fact that the colonists somehow managed to win the
Revolutionary War. The fact that someone from Alabama is a U.S.
citizen is the product of the outcome of another war, almost a century
later. And the fact that native Americans are U.S. citizens is even
more poignantly a product of who had superior weapons and technol-
ogy. Indeed, when one thinks of contemporary examples of secessionist disputes or military occupation, it seems clear that there can be
no convincing argument establishing political obligation that is not
grounded on an underlying territorial argument about legitimate sovereignty over land. The rebel's claim of a right to disobey the government is precisely a declaration that territorial sovereignty is lacking.
And whether the exercise of this right is ultimately successful depends on the coincidental possession of superior force.

International relations theorists have made this argument many
times: the existing distribution of territory is morally arbitrary.[30]
Usually this point is one step toward an argument in favor of international distributive justice. But there is another use for the same
argument, namely, as a point against traditional domestic political
theory. If the existing international distribution of assets is unfair,
then it is unfair to withhold "our" assets from outsiders. But it is also
unfair to use those assets to coerce obedience from those within the

---

[30]See, for instance, Charles Beitz, *Political Theory and International Relations*
(Princeton, N.J.: Princeton University Press, 1979), 136–43.

state. The fact that the government may not legitimately withhold access to territory makes it illegitimate for the government to *condition* access to territory. Thus the international relations argument comes home to roost in domestic political theory. What can be done to an insider because he or she is an insider is linked to the legitimacy of the treatment of outsiders qua outsiders.

This argument seems, on the one hand, to be a commitment to anarchism. It seems to suggest that because national boundaries are unjustifiable, the imposition of political coercion is unjustifiable. Although the argument does strongly tend toward the anarchist position, there may be one way out. That way would be a pragmatic justification for continuing to observe national borders that are the product of force or fraud—even though the existing borders are intrinsically unjustifiable, it is also wrong for practical reasons to try to change them. Such a theory could perhaps be built on a utilitarian philosophy, justifying continued observance of existing borders if they were at least long-standing and stable.

Contemporary political theorists have found it worthwhile to address boundary issues even if they do so for somewhat different purposes. Unlike Simmons, Walzer, and others[31] I focus on the necessity of an underlying theory of territorial sovereignty to any adequate account of particularized political obligation. It makes sense to speak of obligations to a specific nation only if one has a theory of how territory is legitimately acquired or lost.[32] Walzer, in particular, seems to recognize this necessity. But because of the difficulties in defending the national status quo, it is not clear whether a convincing account of national boundaries can be given.

Although a justification of particularized political obligations would require such an account, defense of the vertical thesis itself

---

[31]See, for instance, the application of liberal consent theory to immigration law in Schuck and Smith, *Citizenship without Consent*.

[32]There are rare philosophical discussions of territorial acquisition. See "Perpetual Peace" in *Kant's Political Writings*, Hans Reiss, ed. (Cambridge: Cambridge University Press, 1970), 94. There are also, of course, many discussions of the illegitimacy of territorial aggression and also discussions of the legal aspects of territorial acquisition. See, for example, Robert Jennings, *The Acquisition of Territory in International Law* (Manchester: Manchester University Press, 1963); Percy Corbett, *Law and Society in the Relations of States* (New York: Harcourt, Brace, 1951), chaps. 5–7.

does not require one. The vertical approach to international relations does not depend on proof of either an adequate constituting political theory or an adequate theory of boundaries. If any explanation of national boundaries necessarily rests on the simple entrenchment of the status quo, justification of consequent particularized obligations is a problem for domestic political theorists to address. The vertical thesis, with its integration of political justification and international relations, merely highlights to domestic political theorists the importance of boundaries to the problem of political justification.

Part II

Issues and Implications

Introduction to Part II

The vertical thesis holds that international relations and domestic political activity should be subject to the same requirements of political justification. The thesis is sufficiently abstract to make one wonder where it leads. Perhaps, it will be said, the thesis can be useful once one has made a commitment to a particular constituting political theory—although even that possibility might be doubted. To some degree, there is an existing literature along these lines, for adherents of Rawlsian approaches or of liberal consent theory have tackled particular issues of international relations.[1] But is the more general statement of the vertical thesis any foundation for a theory of international relations? What does the vertical thesis tell us? In particular, one would like to know more about its implications for specific international law problems and the extent to which these implications are different from familiar horizontal conclusions.

Here we seem to encounter a problem in developing the implications of a vertical approach. As a consistency requirement, the vertical thesis by itself seems to tell us very little about specific problems.

[1]For an effort to apply consent theory to immigration law, see Peter Schuck and Rogers Smith, *Citizenship without Consent: Illegal Aliens in the American Polity* (New Haven, Conn.: Yale University Press, 1985). For discussion of the international argument for Rawlsian redistribution, see chapter 6 below.

Only after a commitment to a constituting political theory has been made will the thesis yield specific normative recommendations for particular cases. To develop here the implications of the vertical thesis in conjunction with particular constituting theories would require a catalog of different political theories and their implications. An individual committed to a particular domestic theory need only examine that theory to draw conclusions about international affairs. Not having made such a commitment—and not wishing to defend one—we would here have to survey all domestic theories if we wanted to understand what the vertical thesis would require. Not only would this be an enormous task, but one suspects that it might better be performed by adherents to specific political points of view.

Furthermore, as the last chapter demonstrated, existing theories have paid too little attention to the problem of national boundaries as it affects the issue of domestic legitimacy. If this problem needs to be resolved before a convincing account of domestic obligation can be given, then how much more necessary is a resolution for a complete theory of interjurisdictional affairs? Much work remains before any existing theory can simply be ''applied'' to the international context; it is hard to say precisely what the vertical thesis would require in a particular situation, for the necessary components of the domestic political theory are simply not all there.

What, then, *can* be done to work out the likely implications of a vertical approach? We would like to make use of any plausible existing fragments of political justification, and we would like to compare their international implications with traditional assumptions of international law. We will therefore look at existing general concepts of international law and ask to what extent they are consistent with, or entailed by, existing plausible reasoning about political justifications. We impose here only a minimal condition of plausibility. Compared to the analysis in Part I, this approach moves to a somewhat lower level of abstraction. We ask, What sorts of political justifications might generate the accustomed principles of international law? What would be the influence of particular plausible assumptions of political theory on particular sorts of international problems?

Part 2 attempts in this way to derive at least some rudimentary conclusions from the general foundational assumptions set forth in

Part I. The following chapters pose a series of related issues. How well do certain traditional notions of international law, such as the requirement that states respect one another's sovereignty, fare under the vertical perspective? What about the controversial notions that states may have either affirmative obligations to come to one another's aid or rights to intervene in one another's domestic affairs to prevent human-rights violations? Does the vertical perspective, in other words, generate anything like the usual approach to international theory? When interpreted in line with the vertical perspective, are concepts like sovereignty useful or incoherent and indeterminate? And which political theories, when extended into the international context, would generate traditional notions of sovereignty, humanitarian intervention, and affirmative obligation?

The answers to such questions (to the extent that answers can even be proposed) will be only slightly more concrete than the general program outlined in Part I. The next four chapters deal both with issues that are peculiar to the vertical perspective and with concepts that are common in the traditional horizontal approach. Chapter 4 asks whether there are plausible political theories that would themselves exempt international relations from critical scrutiny. Chapter 5 examines the idea that it is a violation of another state's sovereignty to cause deleterious consequences within that state. In chapter 6, I evaluate the argument that states have affirmative responsibilities to those beyond their borders. In chapter 7, I investigate the issue of humanitarian intervention.

Chapter Four

Self-limiting Political Theories

Why is it usually that only the actions of a state toward a citizen are treated as political relations that must be justified in terms of traditional theory? In the discussion below, I call those relationships that have traditionally been exempt from political evaluation *diagonal* relationships. While they are vertical relations between a state and an individual, they also cross a jurisdictional boundary. This notion is not adequately captured by the word *international* (although I will continue to use the word at times) because it seems to denote relations between the nations themselves—a horizontal relationship. Nor does the word *transnational* really suit present purposes, for it might equally be applied to interjurisdictional horizontal relations between individuals.

Diagonal relations are state-individual relations with international overtones. The thrust of the vertical thesis is that such diagonal relations are simultaneously vertical relations and are for this reason subject to the requirements of political theory. It is not easy to determine which vertical relations are purely domestic and which are diagonal. For instance, some might think that the relationship of a nation to a nonresident guest worker is a domestic vertical relationship, which even under traditional approaches must be justified as a matter of political theory. Others might deny this interpretation, because the relationship is not between a state and its own citizens. Is this relationship diagonal or a purely domestic vertical one?

The most likely characteristics that would distinguish diagonal from domestic vertical relations are that the coerced individual is a noncitizen or that some or all of the coercion takes place in another country. For our purposes, however, we need not be able to draw a precise boundary between diagonal relations and purely domestic vertical relations, because the vertical thesis holds that diagonal relationships are subject to traditional political evaluation. Diagonal relationships are those that the vertical thesis seeks to include as subject to political evaluation and that traditional theory has exempted. In traditional approaches, it is important to be able to draw a line between diagonal and purely vertical relations, for only the latter need be justified politically. Indeed, as remarked earlier, the fact that it is so difficult to figure out where the line should be drawn is a serious problem for traditional theory. For purposes of the vertical thesis, however, diagonal and purely domestic relations are treated the same. The point behind developing this terminology is merely to be able to refer to those actions which traditional approaches did not seek to justify, in order to examine the possible reasons for the exemption.

Even within the vertical thesis itself there are two related ways in which such diagonal coercion of outsiders might be immunized from political evaluation. The first is that when one considers sympathetically the entire enterprise of political justification, one finds that even by its own terms it does not purport to apply legitimacy requirements to diagonal relations. Political theory, as a discipline, is not restricted to state-citizen relationships for some artificial reason. It simply does not purport to impose any requirement of justification on diagonal relations because it does not recognize them as political. The second argument is that particular political theories treat purely domestic relations differently from diagonal ones. It is not the entire enterprise of political justification that differentiates between domestic and diagonal actions, but the particular theories that have been offered to explain state coercion. These two arguments are closely related in that both grow out of political theory itself. Both are consistent with the vertical thesis because interjurisdictional activities are legitimated according to the criteria for standard vertical analysis. They are simply different in their level of generality.

They are overlapping, however, because one's view of what counts as an adequate political justification is likely to be influenced by one's view of what the discipline of political theory purports to apply to, and vice versa. Another way to phrase the relationship between the two arguments is that the former deals with the scope of the question, the latter with the scope of the answer. Political theory, as a discipline, frames the question "how can political coercion be justified?" and political coercion can be interpreted broadly (to include diagonal relations) or narrowly. Particular political theories answer with a set of criteria that must be satisfied for coercion to be legitimate, and these also may be broadly or narrowly phrased.

Such narrow visions of political theory are "self-limiting" because they are limited in their applicability but the limitations come out of what the theory, itself, purports to do. A particular political justification is self-limiting when the requirements that it imposes on domestic vertical coercion are explicitly not applicable to diagonal relations. A vision of the process of political justification, as a whole, is self-limiting when the domain of political theory is understood to include only domestic vertical relations.

If the general discipline is self-limiting, or important individual theories are self-limiting, then the importance of the vertical thesis is reduced. The thesis would still be true, as a formal matter, because all state actions would be subject to the requirements of political theory. But the traditional view that political theory and international relations are separate subjects would also, to a certain extent, be vindicated; it would make sense not to consult political theory when engaging in international actions because political theory does not purport to have anything to say about the subject.

In this chapter we investigate the plausibility of self-limiting political theory. Most traditional scholarship seems implicitly to assume that political theory is self-limiting in one or both of these senses. The general domain of the subject has been thought to be domestic vertical relationships, and the domains of particular solutions to the problem of political justification are also domestic relationships. The vertical thesis challenges that implicit assumption; it suggests that diagonal relationships are not necessarily immune to the requirement of justification. While there may be self-limiting politicial theories, and while the discipline as a whole may be self-limiting, the validity of self-limiting theory cannot simply be taken for granted. The position must be argued for as a matter of political theory itself, since the modest definition of a theory's range comes from within the specific theory or within the discipline of political theory generally.

I will consider some arguments about the scope of political theory generally and of particular political theories in order to evaluate the prima facie plausibility of theories that limit themselves to purely domestic situations. My discussion will not attempt to answer definitively the question of the proper scope of political theory but merely to speculate about the possibility that this question might be answered in terms of domestic actions only.

Recognition

When is an institution acting in a way such that it should be subject to the requirements of political justification? The vertical perspective forces to the surface an issue that tends otherwise to remain submerged. What exercises of official power are appropriately termed political and should accordingly be evaluated by reference to the requirements of normative political analysis? What, in other words, is the proper domain of political theory?

Even in a purely domestic matter the question is sometimes not an easy one. Consider, for example, a problem in official responsibility for individual acts. If an off-duty police officer happens to murder someone, the act would in most circumstances not be considered subject to the requirement of political justification, because it was done in a purely personal capacity. It would raise moral and legal problems but not problems of political justification. On the other hand, under different circumstances the fact that the officer was off duty would not necessarily make the murder a purely personal act. For instance, if a dictatorship deliberately closed its eyes to what its police officers were doing off duty against its political enemies, then this policy could be attributable to the government and therefore in need of justification.

With respect to international relations it is possible to argue that diagonal relations are, like the off-duty murder in the first example, simply not political acts. When a state acts internationally, it is not acting qua state. If its acts are not recognized as political, then they are not subject to critical evaluation according to political theory. To call this a problem of ''recognition'' is to highlight its similarity to another ''recognition'' problem in international relations, namely, whether some particular institution claiming to act on behalf of a nation should be recognized as the nation's government.

When a new government comes into power after a revolution, military coup, or decolonization, the other governments of the world have to decide whether to recognize it. We are all familiar with problems of this sort. At one time there was only one country that the United States called ''China.'' However, the Chinese Communist forces were sucessful in expelling the leaders of that government from mainland China to Taiwan. For quite some time thereafter, the United States refused to recognize Communist China. Pressure eventually grew to accord it official recognition and later to deny official recognition to the expelled government. Comparable difficulties have arisen concerning the status of East Germany and the Palestine Liberation Organization.

Whether to recognize diagonal acts as instances of coercion, like purely vertical acts, is a similar problem. The question is whether some person or group of persons is acting officially, as a government. The difference is that recognizing a new nation operates wholesale rather than retail. One can ask either as a general matter whether the person or group constitutes a government or on a case-by-case basis whether some particular action taken by a member of that group constitutes an official action of the government. As illustrated in the examples of the off-duty police officer, the fact that some of one's actions are official does not mean that all of them are, and it is not always easy to determine which are and which are not.

These examples illustrate that there is a difference between recognizing that something belongs to a particular category and evaluating it according to the standards appropriate to that category. A two-stage process of recognition and evaluation is common even outside political philosophy. Evaluation of an object requires a prior identification of what the object is so that the proper standards of evaluation can be applied. For example, the object that I am sitting on is a chair and not a strawberry. In evaluating the chair, I apply the criteria that I usually apply to chairs. It is comfortable, strong, and reasonably attractive given the limits of my decorating abilities and budget. I don't expect or hope for it to be juicy, fragrant, and tantalizingly sweet.

One should not assume that evaluation is a theoretical matter and recognition is only a factual one. Both are theoretical. In our example of the off-duty police officer, whether the murder is an action of "the government" may implicate factual issues but cannot be answered without recourse to some theory about what "the government" consists of. A government exists because some theory recognizes that it exists; otherwise how would we know that all of those police, judges, legislators, and so on, are part of a common institution? The police officer is a "member" of the government as a theoretical (and not merely a factual) matter, and whether the murder occurred in the officer's official capacity also involves theoretical as well as factual issues.

That recognition is a theoretical problem and not a purely factual one is not unique to politics. When I go to a string-quartet concert I might wish to evaluate the musical ability of the performers. When I ask myself whether they played well or poorly, I do not include in my evaluation an assessment of whether they played well when they tuned up on stage because tuning up is not (in the relevant sense) part of the music. This recognition of what counts as part of the music is not a factual determination but a theoretical one. It reflects my sharing of certain social and aesthetic expectations about what constitutes "the music" at the performance. Someone who knew nothing about Western music or concert going might think that these sounds were the first piece on the program.

It is arguable that diagonal actions of states should no more be subject to political evaluation than tuning up should be subject to music criticism. Whether we apply the evaluative standards of political legitimacy to a state's diagonal relationships depends on whether we recognize the relationships as political in the relevant sense. Three different intuitions potentially explain why diagonal relations have not been recognized as political. All have some appeal and may actually help to account for the fact that diagonal relations have not been evaluated according to political legitimacy. None, however, seems plausible when examined critically. These three arguments base nonrecognition of diagonal activities on, respectively, the type of activity, the location of the activity, and the identity of the coerced individual.

TYPE OF ACTIVITY

The first argument is that a state engages in different types of activities with noncitizens than with citizens and in different types of activities within its territory than outside its territory. Domestically, it collects taxes, establishes a police force and investigates and punishes crimes, provides public services such as hospitals and schools, and so forth. Externally, it may do none of these things. Instead, it may intervene in other state's affairs by use of armed force, supply aid to friendly governments or revolutionary movements, or engage in espionage. These activities are arguably not political in the same sense as the state's domestic actions.

To put the argument a different way, the activities are arguably not coercive in the same sense. They do not require someone to do something. If a state's army invades another nation, it does not require the citizens of the invaded state to obey its laws. It may cause them to flee, burn their villages, or even kill them, but such actions are different from compelling them to obey the state's commands. As Kent Greenawalt has argued in another context, to say that a state is entitled to coerce is not to say that an individual is obligated to obey.[1] Arguably, diagonal relations involve only the former, and domestic relations involve also the latter.

Under this view, if the invading state were to set up a regime to regulate the conquered territory, in effect turning it into a colony, *then* it would perhaps have to satisfy the requirement of political justification. At that point, it would be acting as a government, for it would be engaged in the same sorts of activities that it undertakes at home. Before that point, it could perhaps be condemned on some other ground (such as international morality) but not for failure to justify its actions politically. Only at the point where law was im-

---

[1]Kent Greenawalt, *Conflicts of Law and Morality* (New York: Oxford University Press, 1987), chap. 4.

posed could the state begin to claim that the coerced individuals had an obligation to obey. Until that point, the citizens of the invaded country were enemies, not subjects.

This argument shades off into the argument of special responsibility, which I will consider later, because it involves differentiating among groups of persons as well as types of activities—subjects must be treated according to principles of political justification; outsiders need not be. For now, however, we are focusing on types of activities, not people. The argument is simply that ruling a country is different from other activities that have coercive impact on the country. The former involves promulgation of laws, provision of services, and imposition of political responsibilties. The latter, so the argument goes, involves none of these, and so it is not subject to the same requirements.

There is some reason to believe that such an intuition does indeed account for the common implicit assumption that diagonal relations are not subject to the usual requirements of domestic political justification. The paradigm problems of political obligation concern such topics as payment of taxes, respect for immoral laws, and military sevice in an unjust war. Questions related to these topics do not arise in most foreign-relations problems, because a state does not attempt to make noncitizens shoulder such burdens. Although a state may affect their interests in a negative way, it does not impose an obligation on them to obey the law or otherwise affirmatively support the government.

There is something ironic, however, about using the relatively more lawlike atmosphere of domestic affairs as a reason for the requirement of justification. Admittedly, the state typically treats its citizens in a more lawlike way than it treats noncitizens. It imposes taxes instead of simply confiscating or looting; it tries them for crimes rather than simply shooting or bombing them. But to use this difference as a basis for requiring justification in the domestic case but not the international case is surely backward. The argument suggests that since the requirements of legitimacy are more nearly met in the domestic situation, they need not be met in the international situation at all.

Moreover, the dichotomy is not really so tidy. Ideally, as a domestic matter, the state would not simply murder innocent citizens. But of course, there are cases where states do exactly that. Lawless property seizure and torture arise in the domestic as well as the foreign context. Conversely, although lawlike behavior is more likely to occur in the domestic context, it can also occur internationally, as where the state attempts to apply its tax or regulatory laws to activities in another nation.

What any explanation based on the character of the activity fails to explain is why, once one controls for the type of activity, a difference in treatment is appropriate simply because an activity is domestic rather than international. Presumably we would think that it was illegitimate for a nation to murder its own citizens to gain political advantage. Genocide and political assassination, as domestic policies, are surely ruled out. Why then is slaughter of innocent persons or political assassination immune to political evaluation when it comes to international law? And why shouldn't the legitimacy of such acts be as much a question of political theory as it is in the domestic context? It is easy to concede that different sorts of coercion, of different levels of burdensomeness, carry with them different levels of justification. Recognizing this difference falls considerably short of exempting international conduct from political scrutiny altogether, however.

Perhaps the best that can be said for the argument based on types of activity is the following. At least in the American legal system, some sorts of coercive decisions are implemented by courts, and others are not. Taxes and criminal laws (including punishment for failure to report for military conscription) are subjected to judicial approval. The actions of one's army when it occupies another country typically are not (although the My Lai and Nuremburg trials suggest that judicial investigations even into wartime activities are possible). Because of the fact that they render reasoned opinions, courts are more likely than presidents or generals to offer political-theory justifications.

Thus, those sorts of activities that are enforced through institutions such as courts are more likely to undergo the kind of critical scrutiny in which the question of political justification is posed. Indeed, those private international law problems that are resolved by courts are precisely within the areas of international law where some semblance of political justification has been offered.[2] Perhaps we have become accustomed to seeing such problems (but only such problems) examined from the vantage point of political justification; this familiarity may give rise to expectations about how problems *ought* to be treated. But once made explicit, this assumption seems indefensible. The fact that generals are not typically required to give reasoned written explanations of what they are doing does not mean that their actions need not be justifiable.

EXTRATERRITORIALITY

The second argument about why diagonal relations are not political acts, and need not be evaluated as such, is that a nation is not acting as sovereign when it acts outside its territory. There are two reasons to suppose that this extraterritoriality notion may underlie the failure to recognize diagonal actions as political. The first is an analogy to the scope of sovereignty recognized in a legal doctrine known as sovereign immunity.

In American law, and the law of numerous other nations, official actors are immune from suit without the state's consent.[3] The rationale is explained sometimes by the fiction that the king can do no wrong but usually, more realistically, by the idea that the sovereign that creates the law is entitled to make exceptions to the law for its own conduct. The doctrine of sovereign immunity has constitutional status in the United States due to the Eleventh Amendment. A similar principle is the "act of state" doctrine, which recognizes a form of sovereign immunity in international affairs.[4]

The doctrine is typically limited, however, when the sovereign acts ultra vires. For instance, when a state engages in actions that are impermissible under the federal constitution, it is said that it is no

---

[2]See, for example, the requirement in the Restatement (Revised) of Foreign Relations Law sec. 403 that the application of U.S. law be "reasonable." A.L.I. Restatement (Revised) of Foreign Relations Law (1987).

[3]A discussion of sovereign immunity and its underlying rationale can be found in chapter 3 of Lea Brilmayer et al., *An Introduction to Jurisdiction in the American Federal System* (Charlottesville, Va.: Michie Co., 1986).

[4]See, for example, Banco Nacional de Cuba v. Sabbatino, 376 U.S. 398 (1963).

longer acting as the state; thus sovereign immunity does not apply.[5] Similarly, the act-of-state doctrine grants immunity only when a foreign nation acts within its own territory.[6] The general principle is that a state loses its status as sovereign when it acts beyond its legitimate borders.

The other arguable support for the extraterritoriality argument stems from a notion that might be called "exclusive sovereignty." A state engaged in some activity in another country is operating within that other state's sphere of sovereignty. The other state, after all, is clearly entitled to regulate what occurs within its territory. But if the other state is sovereign in that territory, so the argument goes, the first state cannot also be sovereign, because sovereignty is exclusive and indivisible.

For example, the United States would not send its police into Mexico to pursue a fleeing felon. Instead, it would respect Mexico's sovereignty by requesting extradition. Mexico supplies the police services within its own territory, just as it supplies its citizens with hospitals, schools, and roads. When an official of the United States enters Mexico, he or she ceases to be official and instead operates in a private capacity. Mexico's obviously superior sovereignty over its territory precludes the exercise of American official power. Or so the argument goes.

There are a number of difficulties with the extraterritoriality argument. To the extent that it relies on a notion of exclusive sovereignty, it resembles the argument discussed earlier about types of activities. Admittedly, Mexico is engaging in activities within its territories that are arguably appropriate only for sovereigns. However, this fact does not necessarily mean that because the United States is engaging in different types of activities, it is not acting in a governmental capacity. Unless one rigidly insists that there can be no overlap of sovereign authority, it seems to beg the question to rely on the fact that another country is exercising what are also admittedly sovereign

[5]Ex Parte Young, 209 U.S. 123 (1908).
[6]The Court, for instance, referred in Underhill v. Hernandez, 168 U.S. 250, 252 (1897), to respecting the actions of another state "done within its own territory." See also the *Sabbatino* decision, pp. 400–401.

powers. Why should we assume that only one state is required to justify itself politically?

Such rigid insistence seems implausible. Federal officials enforce laws within the states of the United States, even though those states exercise many of the same police powers that Mexico does (enforcing laws, building roads, providing schools, and so forth) Furthermore, the United States is most definitely engaged in governmental activity in certain international contexts, despite the sovereignty of other states. When it applies its tax or antitrust laws to conduct occurring in other nations, its sovereignty overlaps with that of other countries. "Exclusive sovereignty" is therefore inadequate foundation for the extraterritoriality argument.

More generally, the argument that the state is not acting as a government when it acts internationally seems merely to beg the question. It simply declares diagonal relations exempt from political scrutiny without explaining why. It would be one thing to assert that a state's actions that impinge on other nations are *illegitimate* because they exceed the state's territorial authority. This argument would rest on the state's limited scope of geographical reach. But the thrust of the extraterritoriality argument is precisely the opposite. It is that the criteria for evaluation do not apply to extraterritorial activities. This exemption makes a state's international actions immune to political evaluation, preserving without explanation the talismanic ability of territorial borders to cut off critical scrutiny.

SPECIAL RELATIONSHIP

The third intuition that might explain why diagonal relations have not been subject to the requirements of political justification is that a state has a special relationship with its own citizens. Relationships with outsiders are not political in the same sense and therefore not subject to the requirement of justification. Only citizens can have obligations to support the government, and the requirement of political justification is the correlative of this obligation. A state may coerce outsiders and may affect their interests adversely, but this fact alone does not make the relationship political. Similarly, the fact that a state rather than a private person is engaged in the challenged conduct does not make the action "political" in the relevant sense. Only certain sorts of relationships are subject to the requirement of political justification, and those are the relationships between a state and its citizens.

Such intuitions may indeed account for common sentiments about international theory. For example, we consider the United States a democracy, and by this we seem to mean that decisions are made through electoral processes. Of course, we do not allow Nicaraguans a vote on issues of continuing aid to the contras. How can such an exclusion be squared with the belief that all those affected by a decision should be able to participate in making it?

The explanation probably rests on the special-relationship argument. According to this argument, when we say that the United States is a democratic society, what we mean is precisely that *its citizens* have a right to vote because then the special relationship between the United States government and its citizens is structured democratically. All of those relationships that are recognized as political relationships are democratic: coercion of outsiders need not be justified in democratic terms. The idea that all those whose interests are affected by a decision should be allowed to vote is just high-school civics-class rhetoric. It is no more a violation of democratic principles to invade or bomb a foreign country than it is to dump nuclear wastes into the ocean, so long as the American people want to do these things. We no more have political responsibilities to the Nicaraguans or Vietnamese than we do to the halibut.

The special-responsibility argument can be explained by offering an analogy. It is indisputable that one has special responsibilities to one's own children. This is not to say that one has no responsibilites at all to other helpless young persons, only that those of a parent to his or her own child are distinctive. One acquires these responsibilities only by being in a parent-child relationship, either biological or adoptive. It does not make much sense to try to argue for parental responsibilities outside such a relationship, because our notion of what duties a parent has toward a child grows out of our understanding of what it means to be a parent.

Is it possible that the relationship between a citizen and his or her own state is something of this sort? Perhaps it is our understanding of what the state-citizen relationship is like that gives us our idea of what a state must do to justify its coercive activities. If so, it might make some sense to have one set of criteria for evaluating such relationships but a totally different set of criteria for evaluating relationships with noncitizens. If the United States dropped a bomb on Miami, it would be judged by political criteria; but if it dropped one on Hiroshima, it would be judged (perhaps) by moral criteria; and if it dropped one in the ocean, it would be evaluated by environmental criteria.

The distinctive characteristics of the state-citizen relationship must be demonstrated, however, and not simply assumed. One cannot rely on ethnic, cultural, or religious bonding. Nation states are not necessarily culturally, ethnically, or religiously homogeneous; furthermore, their populations may be hardly distinguishable from those of the foreign states that their decisions affect. We will consider below whether particular theories about particular states might rely on their particular ethnic or religious populations. In the present context, what matters is that although some states perhaps are composed of citizens that all resemble one another and differ from noncitizens, it is not true *as a general matter* that nation states are homogeneous in this way. Given the contemporary mobility of persons, the fact that someone is a citizen may indicate very little other than that he or she wished to enter a state and that the state allowed entry and naturalization. But unless it is somehow possible to show the distinctive bond between the state and its citizens, it seems that the special-relationship argument is merely question begging. It simply asserts that citizens are somehow special, without explaining why.

There are three reasons to doubt the argument. First, the extent to which such relationships can be simply assumed or abandoned seems to make an analogy to familial relationships implausible. Second, there are likely to be some noncitizens that share the cultural or ethnic traits of citizens; why are there not special responsibilities to them? Third, and conversely, it is likely that some citizens do not share these traits. Would we be willing to exempt a state from conformity with requirements of political legitimacy in its treatment of a group of its own citizens? Probably not; indeed, minority groups might deserve greater rather than less protection. But then absence of cultural, ethnic, or religious ties will not explain why actions against outsiders need not be justified.

Such objections to the special nature of the parent-child relationship cannot be made easily, if at all. The specialness of the relationship could be explained in terms of genetic links, the fact that the mother has carried the child in her body, the emotional closeness developed through years of nurturing, and so forth. Children do not suddenly appear, impersonally, as immigrants do. If they did, we would be unlikely to recognize their special claims to the parents' care and attention. The only possible exception is adoption, but even adoption is special because the commitment it involves is modeled on the much more common biological relation. When parents undertake to adopt, they deliberately assume the responsibilities of biological parents.

It is entirely possible that there is something special about the relationship between a state and its citizens. As we noted earlier, the burdens the state places on them are often more extensive and onerous than those it might attempt to place on noncitizens. Membership in a community is different from merely being affected by the community's decisions. Political activity within the community is an exercise in self-definition as well as an effort to influence a process that may have some practical impact on one's life. The fact that membership may be special, however, does not necessarily mean that making decisions that affect outsiders is not also political. Political theory is commonly assumed to be about the legitimacy of state coercion. One might redefine the subject so as to include only group efforts that affect the lives of other members, but such a step would merely declare by fiat that diagonal relations do not count as political. One would still be left with the philosophical problem of why some state may legitimately coerce some particular individual.

Perhaps there are reasons other than these three for limiting the range of political theory to domestic activities and relationships. Type and location of activities and identity of the affected individuals are the explanations that come immediately to mind, but it is possible that there are other and more plausible interpretations that would more successfully differentiate between diagonal and purely domestic vertical relations. Or perhaps there is more to be said for these three arguments than I have realized. The important point is to pose the question. The arguments based on type of coercion, extraterritorial activity, and special relations may as a historical matter be at the root of our traditional reluctance to evaluate diagonal coercion in terms of political legitimacy. When brought into the open and examined critically, however, they do not yet seem very convincing.

PARTICULAR THEORIES

Even if the discipline as a whole is not self-limiting, it is possible that certain constituting political theories might impose few or no legitimacy constraints on diagonal activities. Diagonal relations are recognized as political, in other words, but when the relevant criteria for political evaluation are applied to diagonal relations, they are less likely to be seen as illegitimate. Diagonal relations are not exempt from political evaluation, but unlike domestic relations they always or almost always survive critical scrutiny.

What sort of political theory would be so lenient on governmental actions merely because they crossed national borders? Like the investigation of political theory generally, the investigation of specific theories of political justification focuses on the salient differences between purely domestic and diagonal relations. I noted that the *type* of coercive activity does not necessarily change simply because a relationship is diagonal. However, diagonal actions may be extraterritorial and may involve noncitizens. Although these differences may not exempt diagonal relations from political scrutiny, it is possible that they account for the greater likelihood that diagonal relations will be found legitimate under particular theories of political justification. What particular theories of political justification would recognize a difference between purely domestic vertical relations and ones with extraterritorial implications or consequences for noncitizens?

NONCITIZENS

There are several arguments that a political theory might advance to explain different treatment of citizens and noncitizens. First, one might simply hold a highly ethnocentric or imperialist view of political justification. One might hold that it is the destiny of one's own nation to subjugate the lesser races; a superior culture or religious or ethnic group is entitled to impose its will on inferiors. This is not to state as a general matter that diagonal relations are immune to political evaluation, for other inferior states might still have to legitimate coercion of outsiders. It is only one's own, superior, state that is entitled to coerce outsiders.

A form of contract theory that derived individual rights from the process of contracting itself might be also uncritical of diagonal relations. Now, much modern contract theory assumes that persons have rights by virtue of their status as human beings, prior to their entering into any political society. But it would be possible to propose a contract theory in which persons had no preexisting rights but obtained rights only by entering into social contracts with other persons or with some Leviathan. Such a theory would not grant outsiders any rights because they never entered into a contract, and therefore it would never be illegitimate to coerce them.

What these two examples illustrate is the lengths to which one must go to devise political theories that accord no protection to someone simply because he or she is not a citizen. Our usual assumption is that people have political rights as human beings, despite their racial status or contractual behavior, and this assumption undermines the self-limitations of any particular political theories. Reliance on theories of ethnic or religious superiority, or on rights created by some positive contract, seems implausible. In addition, it is not clear whether there are many existing nations that, practically speaking, fit these constituting theories. As mentioned earlier, few nations are ethnically homogeneous. Still fewer can realistically trace their relations with the present citizenry to any positive contract.

Another variation on the insider/outsider theme is that relations with outsiders are different because noncitizens are protected by their own home states. Citizens are entitled to certain protections—and to deny these would be illegitimate—but noncitizens gain their protection from the norms that regulate relations between their own state and the one that is acting. The difficulty with this argument lies in those cases where a state cannot or will not protect its own nationals, or where the coerced individual is stateless. Where a state chooses not to protect its nationals from diagonal coercion, one must wonder whether this choice is legitimate (in terms of its own constituting theory) and, if it is not, why the individual should be bound by it. If, as seems more likely, the individual's state simply *cannot* protect him or her, then it is hard to see how that state's existence makes it permissible for the acting state to exercise coercion. Why does the existence of the individual's impotent home state legitimate a diagonal act of coercion?

In a related vein, one might argue that a state is entitled to coerce noncitizens because their home states have in some way behaved wrongfully. Perhaps the home state has (diagonally) violated the rights of locals or (horizontally) violated obligations to the acting state. Again, the fact that the coerced individual has a different home state differentiates a diagonal relationship from a purely domestic vertical one. As with the previous argument based on the existence of a home state, there are problems. Why should an individual suffer because of the wrongful conduct of his or her home state? Although one can imagine circumstances in which it would be fair to hold the individuals responsible—for instance, because they supported the obnoxious policy politically—it does not seem that one should simply take as a general presumption that such circumstances exist.

It should nonetheless be recognized that in certain limited sets of circumstances such reasoning might build a horizontal approach to international norms on a vertical foundation. If one's own state is legitimate and makes legitimate concessions to other states about how they might treat its own nationals, the resulting horizontal agreement between states together with the purely domestic vertical relation of a state to its own citizens might provide an answer to the issue of diagonal legitimacy. When the state violates those concessions, it may be fair to coerce the state's citizens (Figure 4). This view suggests an interesting and potentially fruitful approach to horizontal norms of international law. It does not, however, give such norms a

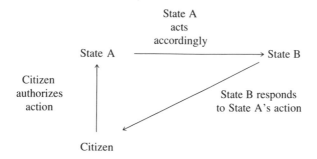

Figure 4. Diagonal relations justified in horizontal and vertical terms

blanket endorsement. Their diagonal legitimacy still depends at a minimum on the legitimacy of the state's attempts to bind its own citizens in their relationship with other states.

EXTRATERRITORIALITY

Just as one might cite the citizen's relationship with his or her own government to explain different treatment of diagonal relationships, one might also point to the fact that diagonal relationships often involve activities in other states. A political theory might treat extra-territorial actions differently because another sovereign also seeks to regulate them. Although I argued above that the existence of an impact on other states would probably not exempt diagonal actions from political scrutiny, there are at least two possible reasons that diagonal actions are more likely to be found justified once a theory of justification is applied.

On the one hand, actions taken outside the state's own territory are less within the state's control. The effectiveness of a state's exercise of power is likely to be at its maximum within its own territory, and more extreme measures might be necessary when acting extrater-ritorially. For instance, it is more difficult to provide humane treat-ment for prisoners of war than for ordinary domestic criminals in prison within the state's own territory. During a war, at or near a battlefield, it is hard to provide prisoners with food and medical care, not to mention impartial adjudication of their claims, because of the general insecurity of the situation. For such reasons, a standard for adjudging humane treatment of prisoners might differentiate between treatment of prisoners at home and treatment in a foreign country. Similar distinctions might be made between espionage and police surveillance over domestic criminals; one can easily imagine other examples.

Admittedly, then, a political justification that treated efficacy as important might differentiate between purely domestic vertical rela-tions and diagonal ones. A theory that required, for instance, that intrusive measures not be used unless they were absolutely necessary to prevent great harm would lead to different results when it was applied internationally and when it was applied domestically. Note however that the important variable is efficacy and not the mere fact that the coercion occurred outside the country. Such a political theory does not grant a blanket license to treat diagonal relationships as qualitatively different, and it would not for this reason explain a reluctance to impose requirements of political justification on diagonal relationships.

A second argument based on the location of events is more likely to excuse diagonal relationships, but it is probably less plausible. The argument is that one should not set out to justify what a state does outside its territory by recourse to the state's *own* theory of political justification because that theory should not be imposed on other nations. Other nations may have different political or cultural conditions, and a state should not treat its own justification as universally true. This leaves unanswered the question of what standard ought to be applied instead, but it does suggest a reason for limiting one's political justification to activities within a nation's territory. The argument purports to respect the unique attributes of other political societies by not treating diagonal relations as domestic vertical ones.

This argument purports to do other societies a favor at the same time that it denies their citizens the protection of its constituting theory. Coerced noncitizens would not claim the protection of a theory of political justification unless it were to their advantage. Denying them this advantage is hard to characterize as deferential. In addition, the coerced individual may in fact come from a culture that provides comparable protections; yet to deny protection merely because a diagonal relationship is involved overlooks the substantial possibility that the other state shares the same basic political values. Cultural relativism may explain why you don't force Moslems to eat pork but it doesn't explain why you napalm them. If a state's constituting political theory guarantees sanctity of the person and other political or civil rights, it is cruelly ironic to deny these protections to those affected by the state's coercion outside its borders on the grounds that one state should not "impose its value choices" on another.

More generally, this argument shows a tendency to confuse the scope of the constituting political theory with the scope of the decisions made pursuant to that political theory. It is one thing to limit the scope of power to enforce a political decision to the persons or activity occurring within a state's own territory. Such a limitation can indeed be explained in terms of deference to the prerogatives of other nations with different cultural or political values. To refuse to extend the requirements of political legitimacy to actions engaged in elsewhere is something entirely different. It extends the state's coercive powers beyond the reach of the political theory that justifies them because the former do not stop at the water's edge while the latter does. If anything, one would expect the legitimacy constraints that limit state action to be more widely applicable than the state action itself.

This search for self-limiting political theory has turned up few promising leads. Of course the fact that the discussion has not suggested a convincing basis for treating diagonal relations differently from purely domestic vertical ones does not mean that none exists. Nor has it thoroughly refuted the ones that have been suggested; it has merely found that at first blush they seem implausible. Probably one cannot address these skeletal suggestions adequately until a proponent has taken the time to develop them into full-fledged theories. While political theory may indeed, by its own terms, exempt diagonal relations, the supporting argument remains to be made.

Chapter Five

Sovereignty and Nonintervention

Perhaps the most frequently invoked concept in the field of international relations is that of sovereignty. A closely related concept is the norm of nonintervention, which holds that states are obligated to respect one another's sovereignty. The concepts of sovereignty and nonintervention have received much attention in the public international law of nation states. In particular, the norm of nonintervention has played a large role in recent political declarations about the rights of sovereign nations. In this context, it has also been referred to as the right of self-determination, which stresses the positive right created by the prohibition against intervention. A particularly strong declaration of this sort is found in the Charter of the Organization of American States:

> *Article 18.* No State or group of States has the right to intervene, directly or indirectly, for any reason whatever, in the internal or external affairs of any other State. The foregoing principle prohibits not only armed force but also any other form of interference or attempted threat against the personality of the State or against its political, economic, and cultural elements.
>
> *Article 19.* No State may use or encourage the use of coercive measures of an economic or political character in order to force the

105

sovereign will of another State and obtain from it advantages of any kind.

Article 20. The territory of a State is inviolable; it may not be the object, even temporarily, of military occupation or of other measure of force taken by another State, directly or indirectly, on any grounds whatever. No territorial acquisitions or special advantages obtained either by force or by other means of coercion shall be recognized.[1]

This norm of nonintervention or self-determination stands as protection not only against territorial occupation but also against colonialism, political subversion, and (when interpreted broadly) economic pressure.

The norm has been justified through an analogy between sovereign actors and individual human beings. A central element of liberal political theory is the autonomy of the individual, that is, the right of self-determination. Nonintervention corresponds to that tenet of political theory, holding that the state may not interfere with an individual's life choices even in order to further that individual's own good. At the extreme, it resembles the libertarian argument for a "minimal state," in the manner of Robert Nozick, which relies on the ideal of personal autonomy.[2] The common thread that links these theories is that a person, and by analogy a state, has a right to control its own affairs. This reliance on the analogy to persons obviously reflects a horizontal bias; sovereignty is perhaps the most important element of the horizontal point of view.

Although sovereignty, as it is usually understood, is quintessentially horizontal, it can easily be reinterpreted in vertical terms. There are three elements in the vertical analysis of the related norms of sovereignty, nonintervention, and self-determination. The first is the vertical limits on the authority of the acting state: it is entitled to exercise coercive power only when it has the theoretical right to do so. The second is the vertical limits on the authority of the state acted on; a state's rights are transgressed only when its legitimate prerogatives are encroached on. The third is a theoretical comparison of the strength of the competing theories of justification in situations where

---

[1]Quoted in Myres McDougal and W. Michael Reisman, *International Law in Contemporary Perspective* (Mineola, N.Y.: Foundation Press, 1981), 166.

[2]Robert Nozick, *Anarchy, State, and Utopia* (New York: Basic Books, 1974).

the vertical authority of two states overlaps. Where both states possess a prima facie vertical claim to assert authority, political theory provides a basis for determining which state possesses the ultimate right to exercise authority when the states' interests conflict.

As we trace out these three elements, we will also uncover a close relationship between the horizontal and the vertical approaches. The vertical analysis is not only a complement to a horizontal one but a necessary complement. The horizontal approach is permeated with notions of political legitimacy that can only be understood in vertical terms. Without a notion of political legitimacy, the horizontal approach is incomplete, functioning more as a rhetorical device than as a tool for analysis.

Each of the three elements of the vertical analysis is necessary to the horizontal approach and is indeed buried beneath the surface of existing horizontal analyses. We will start with the importance of the acting state's legitimate sphere of authority.

Political Legitimacy and the Acting State

The sovereignty norm prohibits intervention or, as one author defines it, "producing internal changes regardless of the wishes of the state intervened in."[3] There can be difficulties, however, with the simple conclusion that state A produced internal changes in state B. It cannot be the case that a state is prohibited from engaging in any actions that produce changes in another state, because in an interdependent world, virtually everything that one state does has impacts on the others. The horizontal approach relies on some ill-defined notion of consequences, changes, or harms produced within a country. However, it offers no objective definition of what counts as a local harm.

There are several respects in which a definition of harm sufficient to violate sovereignty might be controversial. First, a definition must specify which actors are capable of violating state sovereignty. What acts are attributable to the state? For instance, domination by foreign multinational corporations is arguably merely private conduct and not

[3]Charles Beitz, *Political Theory and International Relations* (Princeton, N.J.: Princeton University Press, 1979), 76.

the state's responsibility. The same is true when foreign mercenaries (private citizens) fight in its civil war. One needs a theory of which actions are recognizably political actions of the state before one can accuse the state of violating another's sovereignty. This need can be met by recourse to principles of domestic political justification, for such issues of the public/private status of corporate activities are domestic as well as international.

Second—perhaps more problematic—a definition must specify what sorts of detrimental impact count as impermissible intervention. There are two issues here, one empirical and one normative. The empirical issue concerns whether any factual consequences are really occurring. Often states disagree about whether particular conduct causes harm. For example, states in the vicinity of oceanic testing of nuclear weapons have filed protests against such tests. But whether the testing caused any injury within those states was hotly disputed by the testing nations. Similarly, the dispute over acid rain involves many uncertain factual assumptions. How serious a problem is it? Is it really caused by pollution? It is typically the prerogative of a state to determine similar issues in its domestic legislative capacity, because decisions must be made in the face of uncertainty. Arguably such a determination is a state prerogative in international affairs also—but which state's? It is clear that no decision either way can be made without making an assessment of the likelihood of harm, but the concept of factual injury does not adequately capture controversial estimates of risk.

Furthermore, not all injury is physical in nature; as a normative matter one must decide what sorts of injuries count. It would be arbitrary simply to exclude symbolic injury. For instance, destruction of a religious shrine is a symbolic injury to believers, and it does an injustice to human nature to place such harms categorically below physical consequences.[4] Flight through another nation's air space is a classic violation of sovereignty that seems not to involve any tangible injury. Although insistence on factual harm is far too restrictive, it

[4]See, for example, "Indian Religious Freedom and Governmental Development of Public Lands," *Yale Law Journal* 94 (May 1985): 1447, discussing protection of religious shrines. Intangible harms have been recognized as giving rise to Article III case or controversy jurisdiction. See, for example, Sierra Club v. Morton, 405 U.S. 727 (1972), discussing harm to the environment.

will not do simply to recognize any harm as a violation of sovereignty. In the first place, an injury might be experienced simply because the injured party is hypersensitive. Now, characterizing an injury as hypersensitive obviously rests on a value judgment. Hypersensitivity means that the injury suffered does not rise to the level of political, legal, or moral recognition and protection. But unless we are willing to rule out certain injuries as simply excess sensitivity, an injury in fact can be manufactured in every case.

Particularly problematic is the question whether economic injury can count as a violation of sovereignty. The OAS declaration quoted at the beginning of this chapter treats economic domination as a violation of sovereignty. Are all economic harms violations of sovereignty? What if Japan effectively competes with the United States in the worldwide auto market, thereby damaging American manufacturers? Surely Japan does not violate U.S. sovereignty. Another example is the harm caused by unequal distributions of wealth. Assume that three nations, A, B, and C, all possess equal wealth. Now B and C engage in mutually advantageous trading, which makes them better-off than they were and thus better-off than A. Has A been harmed? Has its sovereignty been violated? If not, then why do many persons assume that an unequal distribution of wealth is harmful to the less well-off? What about the envy its citizens experience?

Such questions are avoided—or at least redefined—under the vertical approach. They are avoided in that the responsibility for providing answers is assigned to the domestic political theorists. Some impacts on individuals must be justified; others need not be. Whether justification is necessary is determined according to the relevant constituting political theory. In place of poorly focused arguments about intervention are questions of political justification. These may involve difficult normative issues or controversial factual assumptions, but at least there is a tradition of political philosophy to structure the discussion.

The problem of defining local harm sufficient to count as a violation of state sovereignty parallels a classic dilemma in liberal moral theory.[5] The liberal would like to say that anything one does that affects no one else is one's own private business. The state has no

---

[5]See Joel Feinberg, *Harm to Others* (New York: Oxford University Press, 1984).

right to regulate private religious beliefs or deviant sex between consenting adults or driving motorcycles without helmets, because the harm these activities may cause is limited to the persons that engage in them. But it is simply too easy to manufacture consequences. A lot has been written about problems in factually verifying the "impact" of consensual activities. Does toleration of homosexuality *really* cause Western civilization to crumble? Does the state *really* have an added welfare burden of supporting paraplegic ex-motorcyclists who weren't wearing helmets? Either of these consequences, if factual, could give the state the right to intervene.

But the factual problems may not be as intractable as the theoretical ones. Who is to say what counts as impact? Does it count as impact that it sickens me beyond belief that the people next door engage in extramarital sex? What if their behavior causes me to have ulcers or migraines? Is it an intrusion on my liberty that I am restrained from doing what I can to stop this disgusting activity? It takes a powerful moral theory to distinguish "real" impact from "phony" or inconsequential impact. Such a theory involves a value-laden differentiation among impacts to determine which ones an individual ought to be required to tolerate. Much more is needed than a principle against violating the autonomy of others, whether they be states or people. Because there must be rules for defining what counts as an impermissible violation, norms of nonintervention and sovereignty cannot be manufactured out of thin air. The vertical thesis at least provides an additional source of guidance, namely, domestic political theory.

Political Legitimacy and the State Acted Upon

One vertical interpretation of the norm of state sovereignty might therefore be that whether a violation has occured depends on whether the acting state has exceeded the scope of its constituting political theory. The harms that are forbidden are those that must be justified under domestic political theory but for which no justification can be given. The vertical equivalent of the horizontal nonintervention requirement would be the simple insistence that a state limit its international actions to what it could justify under its domestic political theory. Vertical analysis does impose such a requirement; but this requirement by itself does not completely capture the norm of nonintervention. In particular, it does not capture a distinctively horizontal aspect of that norm—that the acting state is intruding on the prerogatives of other nations. The simple vertical requirement that a state not exceed the scope of its legitimate authority does not recognize the special fact that a violation occurs at the expense of another state.

This feature of the nonintervention norm is the one that horizontal accounts take seriously: one state suffers because of another state's actions. Yet, as we will see, this apparent horizontal aspect of the nonintervention norm can be accommodated within a vertical analysis without much difficulty. In addition, the horizontal account of the second state's rights needs to be supplemented with some notion of political legitimacy.

Even a horizontal analysis of state sovereignty and nonintervention requires at least a primitive notion of what constitutes legitimate political action by the acted-upon state. The norm of nonintervention does not require that one state be entitled to pursue ruthlessly its own interests, protected from all interference from other states. States sometimes are entitled to thwart one another's plans. It is not a violation of another state's sovereignty simply to do something that the other state does not like or something that interferes with its achievement of one of its goals. Only interference with its legitimate prerogatives, or internal affairs, is typically counted as impermissible intervention.

For example, assume that one state invades another and a third state comes to the invaded state's rescue. Is the third state's action a violation of the invading state's sovereignty? It seems unlikely; even if there are other grounds for protest, the assistance hardly seems objectionable as a violation of the invading state's sovereignty. However, if instead of invading another state, the state is attempting to put down a domestic rebellion and outsiders come in to support the secessionist movement, their intervention might very well be counted as a violation of its sovereignty. The state is being interrupted in the management of its internal affairs.

As this example suggests, even according to the horizontal view, whether there is a violation of the acted-upon state's sovereignty depends on whether the interference is within the scope of that state's legitimate power. The required theory of which affairs are internal and which external is itself a vertical theory, for it poses the question of the scope of the acted-upon state's legitimate authority. Furthermore, it seems clear that this notion of sovereignty must be defined by the state's scope of authority to rule, in the traditional political theoretical sense. It cannot be that the sovereignty that is protected is defined in horizontal terms, because to define it in horizontal terms would make the concept of sovereignty circular or vacuous.

Imagine what a horizontal account of what is protected would look like. Instead of saying, in vertical terms, that what is protected is the state's right to regulate persons, places, and occurrences, one would say that what is protected must be defined in terms of the horizontal relationship between states. The scope of authority would be the set of things with which other states are not supposed to interfere. But such a definition of what is protected would tell us nothing. It would merely say that one state is not supposed to interfere with those activities of another state that are supposed to be protected from outside interference. To give content to the concept of state sovereignty, therefore, one must turn to vertical notions, which define a state's protected activities in terms of its vertical scope of regulation of persons and territory.

In exactly such a vein, some contemporary writers have founded their arguments for the autonomy of states on theories of liberal democratic or communitarian values. For example, Beitz argues that not all states are automatically entitled to autonomy rights; whether they can claim such rights depends on whether they are the proper sorts of states—in his view, states that protect the autonomy rights of their citizens.[6] Walzer develops a theory of political communities that takes seriously the question why a state has collective rights.[7] He clearly recognizes and develops the link between political theory and the sovereignty rights of states. Both authors demonstrate in their arguments how political justification is central to a concept of state autonomy, although the justifications on which they focus are different from one another and also from simple territorial assumptions. The state's protection from intervention is limited to its legitimate activities, defined according to political theory.

[6]Beitz, *Political Theory*, 121.
[7]Michael Walzer, *Just and Unjust Wars* (New York: Basic Books, 1977), especially pt. 2.

While both Beitz and Walzer are consistent in this regard with vertical analysis, the point that the acted-upon state must be acting within its legitimate sphere is more general than the arguments they make. The vertical approach is not a consequence of any particular political theory, such as liberal democracy or communitarianism. It is a general statement about the relationship between political justification and international relations; a violation of the acted-upon state's sovereignty involves interference with some activity that the acted-upon state had a right to engage in. This general point holds regardless of one's choice of political justification. Indeed, the sovereignty norm takes a rather different shape depending on the particular justification employed. One might, for example, rely on a highly territorial theory of political justification, under which a state has virtually complete rights to govern some geographical area. Such a justification gives rise to what should be a relatively familiar interpretation of the nonintervention norm, namely, that a state is protected from other state's efforts to influence what goes on within its own territory.

This observation about the importance of the acted-upon state's political justification to its sovereignty claim leads to our revising the initial approximation of a vertical interpretation of the norm of nonintervention. Rather than ask only about the acting state's political justification, one must ask also about the political justification of the state acted upon. The revised interpretation would be that a state violates the norm of nonintervention when it exceeds its political authority in a way that simultaneously encroaches on the legitimate prerogatives of another state. This interpretation may be more accurate than the first, but it is still not quite complete. It fails to account for cases where the constituting political theories overlap.

Overlapping Authority

The purpose of the norm of state sovereignty is to ensure a state's control over activities within the scope of its own legitimate sphere of authority, free from interference from other states. It is for this reason—to protect state autonomy—that intervention is prohibited. The problem with simply prohibiting impingement on another state's legitimate sphere is that there are areas of concurrent legitimate authority. It is possible that two states' scope of justified power might overlap.

Where constituting political theories overlap, the situation appears symmetric. It is not clear which state's sovereignty should give way. This symmetry has been pointed out in the literature on law and economics. In a celebrated article, Ronald Coase attacked Pigovian economics, which had proposed that a state internalize the costs that an industry imposed on those in its vicinity.[8] Assume that a factory releases pollutants into the air, which cause damage to crops growing on a nearby farm. Pigou claimed that the state should internalize this cost by penalizing or taxing the factory to the extent that it caused damage.

As Coase pointed out, however, one might as easily say that the owner of the farm had caused the damage. If the farmer had chosen instead to grow a different crop, the damages might have been averted. In fact, the farmer might have chosen not to grow any crops at all, and thus the damage to the crops was caused as much by the decision to grow crops as by the decision to pollute. The same reasoning can be applied when it is sovereignties, rather than land-holdings, that are at issue. If state A engages in an activity that injures state B, then the harm is caused as much by state B's vulnerability as by state A's action. Furthermore, it may injure state A to be unable to take the action. The legitimate autonomy of one state or the other must give way. But which?

Without an additional norm to make that choice, the symmetry problem is intractable under the horizontal approach wherever a problem has practical ramifications for the internal affairs of more than one state. One or the other state will be frustrated in its efforts to exercise control over its internal affairs. It is impossible for both states to have complete sovereignty over their domestic situations. If taken literally, the norm of nonintervention would mean that each state must defer to the other; neither can take action. The inability to act itself frustrates self-determination, however. Conversely if both states are allowed to act, then each violates the autonomy of the other.

Internationally, many actions are undertaken in order to procure

[8]Ronald Coase, ''The Problem of Social Cost,'' *Journal of Law and Economics* 3 (October 1960): 1.

benefits within the state's own domestic sphere. Trade policies are designed to alleviate local unemployment, arms embargoes are designed to please local constituents, and so forth. A flat prohibition on intervention would make all courses of action with international implications impermissible. Clearly this would involve an infringement on the autonomy of the state contemplating action. The infringement comes not from the actions of any other state but from the operation of the nonintervention norm itself. Furthermore, such a prohibition may infringe on efforts toward apparently legitimate goals of the acting state, such as reducing unemployment, not just goals that a state was not entitled to pursue anyway.

The horizontal interpretation of the sovereignty norm provides no way to break the impasse. Perhaps both states should be thwarted from acting where spheres of authority overlap, but such a solution leaves some areas completely immune to regulation. Not only does the solution seem pointless but it infringes unnecessarily on the autonomy of both states at once. The infringement is unnecessary because surely it would be better to allow at least *one* of the states to achieve its goals, even if both cannot. Of course, if one looks behind the nonintervention rhetoric, one finds that horizontal analysis offers just this solution. Horizontal reasoning does not and cannot prohibit all actions where states have overlapping spheres of legitimate authority.

Assume, for example, that a citizen of one nation visits another temporarily. One might recognize two potential sets of obligations: the visitor's obligations to the home state and to the state visited. One might take the position that the visited state has no right to regulate the conduct of the visitor, because regulation would interfere with the prerogatives of the home state. A loose definition of what the sovereignty norm requires, such as the formulation at the beginning of this chapter, could conceivably be read to protect a state's relations with its citizens, free from interference by other nations.

But such blanket prohibitions against state action are not usually thought to be entailed by the prohibition against intervention. The reason is that where spheres of authority overlap, we find ways to rank them. In the above example, we would usually hold the claim of the state of temporary location to be superior to the claim of the state of residence. The state of location does not impermissibly intrude upon the sovereign prerogatives of the home state by requiring the visitor to respect the laws; but arguably there would be a sovereignty violation if the home state sought to regulate its citizens' actions while they were elsewhere. I do not mean that this is always the case (one might perhaps have a different rule for diplomats) or that there is any particular reason why one political theory (in this case, territoriality) should trump the other (here, citizenship).

The point, rather, is that the way to resolve the overlap of legitimate authority is precisely the same as the way to determine the extent of authority in the first place. That way is through philosophical analysis of the strengths of the competing political justifications. Perhaps on closer scrutiny it will indeed appear that territoriality expresses a tighter connection, a more compelling basis for political obligation, than membership in a national community. Perhaps the opposite. Or perhaps it depends on the circumstances. The question is not so very different from analysis of competing ethical obligations or of competition of a political with a religious obligation. Examination of the underlying political justification is the way to determine which state's sovereignty prevails when more than one state possesses a prima facie claim to assert authority.

This, then, is the third respect in which a horizontal account depends on vertical analysis. Not only must one analyze the vertical claims of the two states competing to influence some international situation, but one must also be prepared to evaluate them comparatively in case of conflict. Like the previous two elements, this vertical element is implicit already in the notions of sovereignty and nonintervention. A state is prohibited, under a vertical analysis, from exceeding its own legitimate sphere of authority, as defined by its constituting political theory. When it does exceed its authority and encroaches on the more legitimate prerogatives of another state, it violates that state's prima facie sovereignty. Even if it would be within its usual domestic prerogatives (if no other state were involved), it violates the sovereignty of another state if it infringes on a superior claim to govern.

This vertical account of state sovereignty and nonintervention should seem reasonably comfortable to those familiar with the traditional horizontal framework. Its conclusion is not very different. Indeed, it merely builds on the vertical elements already present in more traditional accounts. By making them more explicit and linking them to the existing literature of political justification, international protection for state sovereignty receives additional theoretical support. Vertical analysis is a securer foundation than a horizontal analysis derived from the traditional analogy between states and autonomous human actors.

Chapter Six

Affirmative Duties

The argument that a state is obliged to justify all of its international coercive actions according to its own domestic political theory is clearly based on the concept of negative liberty. Persons have certain rights by which they are allowed to be left alone; there are areas of their private lives into which the state may not intrude without adequate justification. What must be justified, under this view, is state interference with an individual's private life. Nonintervention need not be justified because it is not coercive.

This view is, of course, debatable. A starving individual may take no solace from the fact that the government did not invade her free-speech rights or appropriate her property without compensation. Its very passivity in her particular case may be the focus of her complaint. Both because the state is involved in creating the social environments in which we find ourselves and because lack of action can be as deleterious as active interference, it is entirely plausible that failure to act must in some circumstances also be justified and that affirmative assistance may sometimes be required.

The implications of this difference in perspective for international law are not hard to discern. To this point, we have implicitly spoken as though only affirmative acts of foreign policy must be justified. Only such actions were characterized as coercive. The view that failures to act might also be in need of justification would create an affirmative duty to assist persons or states on the other side of the jurisdictional border where no justification could be given. The question, then, is how such affirmative duties fit within a vertical analysis.

The issue is of much more than academic importance. Of particular foreign-policy concern, for example, is the distribution of resources between developed and developing countries.[1] To what extent does the United States have famine-relief obligations, for example? Are obligations simply vague notions of charity or firm requirements of principle? Affirmative duties might also be found in less life-threatening situations. Under what circumstances, for example, might the United States be obliged to extend the advantages of suit in its courts and under its laws to victims of accidents in other countries?[2] These subjects have attracted a great deal of attention in the philosophical literature of international law. There is increasing support for the argument that affirmative duties beyond political borders exist.

I do not attempt here to make a choice between the domestic negative-liberty and the affirmative-duty positions. Rather, my purpose is to examine the extent to which the belief in international affirmative duties is either consistent with, or a corollary of, the vertical thesis that states are limited internationally by their domestic constituting political theories. In other words, does a domestic theory providing affirmative duties necessarily require affirmative responsibilities in the international context? To what extent is the dispute about the existence of international affirmative duties essentially an argument about domestic political theories, that is, about whether they impose even a domestic obligation of affirmative assistance?

Sources of Affirmative Duties

There are several obvious sources of the intuition that affirmative duties are owed to other nations. The first and perhaps most obvious

[1]See, for example, Peter Singer, "Famine, Affluence, and Morality," in Charles Beitz, Marshall Cohen, Thomas Scanlon, and A. John Simmons, eds., *International Morality* (Princeton, N.J.: Princeton University Press, 1983); Henry Shue, *Basic Rights: Subsistence, Affluence, and American Foreign Policy* (Princeton, N.J.: Princeton University Press, 1980); Brian Barry, "Humanity and Justice in Global Perspective," in J. Roland Pennock and John Chapman, eds., *Ethics, Economics, and the Law* (New York: New York University Press, 1982).

[2]On applying American law, see Henry Shue, "Exporting Hazards," in Peter

is the sense that today's impoverished nations are by and large ones that were historically oppressed by the nations currently enjoying higher standards of living. The cause of the needs they experience, in other words, is the prior wrongful actions of developed nations, who now (it would be argued) have obligations to assist.[3]

This argument is, historically speaking, entirely plausible. Western imperialism certainly exploited some peoples in ways that cry out for redress. As a theoretical matter, however, such arguments do not establish a general obligation to assist other nations in need. For one thing, whether the cause of present impoverishment was imperialism is historically contingent. There are certainly other possible causes of poverty, such as war, lack of natural resources, or natural catastrophe (earthquakes, drought, and so forth). For another, arguments about prior wrongs would require reparations even if the wronged society had recovered economically and could not make a need-based claim. The argument about exploitation is an argument of corrective justice, which is different and separable from the position that affirmative duties are owed simply because of the recipient's current need. It happens that the two arguments often lead to similar results given the current international state of affairs. Even within a particular political theory, corrective justice does not create affirmative duties generally.

Somewhat similar to the argument based on corrective justice would be one based on an affirmative agreement between states. For instance, two states might agree to come to each other's assistance in time of need (invasion, crop failure, natural disaster, or whatever). This is not an argument of corrective justice (a "tort" argument) but one based on promise (a "contract" argument). It is similar, however, in that it does not support an argument for general affirmative assistance.

The most likely support for a general duty would seemingly come from comparable domestic obligations in the constituting political theory itself. In the current debate about negative liberties and affirmative duties, some hold that with regard to domestic matters states

---

Brown and Henry Shue, eds., *Boundaries* (Totowa, N.J.: Rowman and Littlefield, 1981).

[3]For a discussion of such "historical" arguments in favor of assistance, see Judith Lichtenberg, "National Boundaries and Moral Boundaries," in Brown and Shue, *Boundaries*.

need only justify active coercion, and others hold that with regard to domestic matters failure to intervene can also be suspect. The domestic question is whether there are affirmative responsibilities toward persons that are subject to the state's coercive powers. But if a state is justified by a constituting political theory that imposes affirmative duties, then the duties might carry over into the international context. Even persons not subject to a state's active coercion might have a right to affirmative assistance that would be comparable to the rights of persons that *are* subject to the state's coercion.

In asking about the existence of affirmative obligations toward those beyond the state's coercive reach, we might differentiate between two related questions. First, to establish obligations to outsiders, is it *necessary* to show that there are affirmative obligations to insiders? Second, is it *sufficient* to show that there are obligations to insiders? The first question seems relatively easy. Absent arguments of reparations or promises to assist, it is hard to imagine why an outsider would possess rights in situations where an insider would not. If outsiders have affirmative assistance rights, then insiders most likely possess them also.

Indeed, it seems implicit in the way that arguments have been made about affirmative international duties that comparable duties would also exist with regard to citizens. Duties to outsiders depend on duties to insiders. Charles Beitz's argument in favor of affirmative duties, for instance, is that John Rawls's principles of justice ought to be *as applicable* to the international context as to the domestic scene.[4] Frequently it is not necessary to make the premise about domestic duties explicit. For instance, in arguing in favor of famine relief it may seem necessary to posit explicitly that the United States has sufficient wealth to help out, but it is not necessary to posit explicitly that U.S. citizens have a right to receive assistance should they also be on the verge of starvation, for domestic assistance may merely be taken for granted. Anyone who found the affirmative-duty argument persuasive in the international context would probably find it convincing domestically as well.

In this sense, then, the domestic and international affirmative-duty

---

[4]Charles Beitz, *Political Theory and International Relations* (Princeton, N.J.: Princeton University Press, 1979).

arguments are congruent: the latter is a necessary condition for the former. Someone who denies that such duties exist domestically is unlikely to be persuaded that they exist internationally. To convince such a person of international duties requires an argument over domestic political theory. What, then, about the converse? Does a demonstration that affirmative duties are owed to those subject to the state's coercion compel the conclusion that they are owed to outsiders also? Is the duty to insiders a *sufficient* condition?

The strongest argument for sufficiency, it seems, rests on notions of equality and nondiscrimination. Once domestic rights were convincingly shown, it would be claimed that duties were equally owed to all human beings. We made a similar argument in a different context: the limitations on what a state may do domestically are applicable also internationally. Negative rights extend across borders. With regard to restrictions on the right to coerce—that is, the limits on what a state may do—we argued that the mere interposition of a jurisdictional border is not enough to render limitations irrelevant. Now the same argument can be made with respect to affirmative duties; that is, they also apply to outsiders.

Whether this argument is persuasive will depend on the underlying rationale of the affirmative rights that are recognized domestically. If the rationale predicates affirmative rights simply on one's status as a human being, then the theory seems as pertinent in the international context as the domestic context. But are all theories of affirmative rights necessarily based on such a general conception? Or might affirmative rights be embodied in a domestic political theory that is pertinent to insiders but not outsiders, for example, a theory that differentiates between those subject to state coercion and those not subject to state coercion? What legitimate difference would it ever make that a necessitous individual had no obligation to obey the state from which he or she sought assistance?

The question is whether political theories might be partially self-limiting. We said earlier that a political theory was self-limiting if it purported not to apply to diagonal actions either because they were simply not political or because they were always legitimate. We found no convincing reason that political theory as a whole was self-limiting. Here we are speaking only about a certain aspect of political theory, namely, the part that provides an obligation of affirmative assistance. It is possible that this aspect of the theory by its own terms applies only to domestic and not to diagonal relations. The very rationale for recognizing an obligation does not, in other words, extend to international situations.

There are at least two possible arguments to the effect that those exempt from the state's coercion are not necessarily entitled to its assistance. The first is that assistance is the quid pro quo for submission to state coercion. The second is that because of the constraints on a state's ability to protect the long-term well-being of persons over whom it may not exercise coercive power, a general duty to assist cannot be imposed fairly.

Coercion and Assistance

The argument that coercion and assistance are quid pro quo should look familiar. Its essence is that obligations and benefits compensate for one another. The usual context in which such an argument is made is the reverse of the situation under discussion: when one has received the benefits of a state's activities, one is obliged to take on a fair share of the support of them. The usual import of the quid-pro-quo argument, in other words, is to establish an obligation to obey. As a theory of political obligation, the quid-pro-quo argument has serious weaknesses, which I have argued in this book and others have argued elsewhere.[5] We will return below to benefits as a basis for coercion; here we are making the argument in a somewhat different form: a person who is not subject to a duty to obey is not entitled to claim benefits from the state. What remains to be seen is whether this version of the quid-pro-quo argument is stronger than the other.

One serious weakness in the argument seems to be the difficulty of showing that a particular state has a right to the resources it currently possesses. For example, one might say that because a foreign earthquake victim was under no obligation to obey American law, he or she has no right to claim a portion of U.S. wealth. But we must ask why it is "our" wealth. The natural resources the United States

[5]For a criticism of the benefits argument, see A. John Simmons, *Moral Principles and Political Obligations* (Princeton, N.J.: Princeton University Press, 1979), chap. 5, "The Principle of Fair Play," and chap. 7, "Gratitude."

enjoys are something of a stroke of good luck; why are we entitled to withold them from those in need? As we saw in an earlier chapter, the need to have already shown sovereignty over resources is indeed one reason that the quid-pro-quo argument broke down as a justification for political obligation: the quid-pro-quo argument presumes the very sovereignty it seeks to explain.

The difficulty of demonstrating a state's sovereignty over resources does not, however, have the same effect on the quid-pro-quo argument in the present context. The argument merely reiterates what we said earlier about the necessity of a boundary theory for all political justification. All theories of political justification rely implicitly on a prior notion of sovereignty, in this case the sovereignty of the United States over its resources. Thus, to say that the United States has not shown a right to monopolize its natural resources is to argue that an adequate constituting political theory has not been shown. This is a good argument when the issue is establishment of sovereignty. But the question under consideration here assumes that an adequate political theory has already been shown. It merely asks whether the state is obliged to bestow benefits on those who are beyond the reach of its legitimate coercion. It is circular to rely on sovereignty over resources to prove sovereignty, but it is not circular to rely on sovereignty that has already been proven to deny an obligation to assist.

The point here is not to demonstrate that the quid-pro-quo argument is true but only that it is plausible. Whether it is actually convincing is a question of domestic theory—its plausibility depends on the basis for finding affirmative rights in the first place. The question is whether a theory might plausibly provide rights for insiders but not for outsiders. Here I merely mean to suggest that a domestic theory might have such self-limiting features, that they would have international implications, and that the way to argue over the international issue is to take on the premises underlying the domestic theory. For such purposes, only plausibility need be shown, and it does seem at least plausible that a domestic theory might include such reasoning.

One of the political theories that could give rise to a quid-pro-quo argument is the contractarian approach. Persons make themselves vulnerable in certain ways when they subject themselves to state coercion. Certain forms of self-help (theft or fraud) may no longer be available. For this reason, it might be argued that we exchange our right to engage in self-help for a guarantee of assistance from the state. Territorially limited, affirmative duties on the part of the state might therefore arise out of a political theory based on contractarian reasoning.

The quid-pro-quo argument is also compatible with certain arguments based on hypothetical consent. Roughly speaking, one might justify political obligation on grounds of the fairness of a state's institutions, with fairness defined in terms of the likelihood that individuals would adopt them if they did not know in advance which position in society they would occupy. This argument is, of course, a simplified version of an argument promoted by John Rawls.

A simplified Rawlsian theory might support the quid-pro-quo argument because during a hypothetical earlier opportunity to reflect on establishing a state, individuals would reason that they had no motivation to set up institutions that would redistribute wealth to persons beyond the coercive reach of the state.[6] Whatever the likelihood that they would agree to redistribute wealth among themselves (and the likelihood of such agreement, of course, is a controversial aspect of the Rawlsian position), they would know that redistribution to those beyond the state's power would be of no conceivable advantage. From such a perspective, it would be sensible to agree to assist only those who were subject to an enforceable duty to reciprocate.

In response, it would probably be said that such a simplified Rawlsian perspective would mandate redistribution across boundary lines when there was some set of institutions capable of requiring reciprocation. In such circumstances, other nations would also adopt principles of mutual assistance, because they would stand to benefit, and we would all be better-off with such a system of global redistribution. Further, there might be obligations to work to set up a global cooperative network. This response changes the nature of the problem, though. We started with an assumption simply of states, and asked whether they are obliged to assist individuals who are beyond their coercive reach. It cannot be an adequate answer that if there were a superstate, with individuals from all nations subject to its

---

[6]Cf. Beitz, *Political Theory*, pt 3, sec. 2, "Entitlements to Natural Resources."

coercion, then that state would fairly redistribute wealth from one nation to another. Perhaps we would all be better-off under such a system; perhaps we would not. Perhaps we all ought to work toward establishing one—but in the meantime, do we have an obligation to redistribute wealth? One cannot address the problem of obligations to those beyond the state's coercive reach by simply hypothesizing a system in which everyone is subject to coercion. The question remains whether given the existing limits on coercive action, the duty to assist extends beyond them.

The quid-pro-quo argument thus raises at least some healthy obstacles to the argument about a general duty of assistance. So long as we assume that there must be a justification for redistributive actions by states, it may be hard to justify taking wealth away from insiders and putting it to use in a way that will be of no benefit to them. Whether these difficulties are fatal to the argument for affirmative duties is another matter. As should be clear from the links between the quid-pro-quo argument and the various domestic political theories, one's view toward the argument is likely to be a function of one's beliefs about domestic political justification.

In other words, if one espouses a constituting political theory that provides affirmative duties but is based on a simplified Rawlsian foundation, it may be reasonable to deny a general obligation to assist persons not subject to the coercive power of the state. The same is true if one sees obligation and receipt of benefits as quid pro quo for one another. Whether duties toward outsiders exist depends not only on whether the constituting political theory provides affirmative benefits as well as negative liberties, but also on whether the rationale for these affirmative benefits applies to all human beings generally. An observer who accepts self-limiting political theories founded on reasoning that is not universally applicable in this way may deny that duties across borders can be shown.

Lack of Control and Effective Assistance

In contrast to the quid-pro-quo argument, the second argument focuses on the difficulties of providing effective relief: it may not be realistic or fair to impose a duty to help when the donor has no control over the recipient's actions. Where the recipient engages in counterproductive or short-sighted activities, it will be excessively costly or even impossible to assist with long-range solutions. The inability to control the actions of those not subject to state coercion thus negates any duty to provide assistance.

It is all too easy to think of examples of this sort of problem. Some instances of impoverishment involve nations with birthrates that have outstripped their capacities to provide food, with corrupt governments that misappropriate relief funds, or with unsound environmental policies that destroy long-run resources for short-run gains. This is not to say that developed nations are astute environmentally, or have honest and efficient governments and no problem of overpopulation. Indeed, among the most developed countries are those that are the most wasteful. Rather, the point is that they have evolved their own policies toward such problems, and they handle them as they like and then bear the consequences. If they were to ask for aid, then their inability to act in an environmentally responsible way or control waste or a high birth rate would be relevant. The issue is whether it is obligatory to provide economic assistance to states that insist on pursuing counterproductive policies and that may even strongly resent any efforts to suggest or require internal changes as a condition of assistance.

Similar problems arise between persons, or between a state and a person with regard to areas into which the state is supposed not to intervene. For example, public assistance in the domestic context raises troubling moral issues when recipients of assistance decline to seek education or employment, or continue to give birth to children whom they cannot adequately support. Because in American culture there is a belief that an individual has a sphere of privacy into which the government ought not to intrude even when it provides economic assistance, the duty to assist is coupled with an absence of coercive power. Most of us, for instance, would not condition continued welfare on submission to sterilization or abortion. The public resentment provoked by this combination of lack of coercive power and obligations to assist is evident; those who pay for public assistance complain that poor people shouldn't keep having illegitimate children, shouldn't spend their food money on convenience foods, and so forth. The pressure mounts for intrusion into areas that ideally would be kept private. The tension between the absence of a right to coerce and the presence of a duty to assist is unavoidable.

This combination also raises questions, in both the domestic and the international context, about the obligations of the recipient of assistance. If we assume that unequal distribution of wealth is undesirable, then we may be inclined to adopt some redistributive scheme in order to remedy the inequality. All such schemes impose burdensome obligations on those who must give up their wealth for redistribution. But are there corresponding obligations on the recipients? Presumably they should have equal responsibilities to engage in activities that reduce the disparity. They should be prohibited from taking any action that contributed to their own impoverishment. While imposing such obligations and using state coercion for enforcement might involve intrusions into areas otherwise regarded as private, wealth redistribution likewise involves intrusion into the interests of those with resources.

These arguments are likely to be deeply controversial, but they at least seem to offer plausible reasons that a state might not have a duty to assist in those situations where it has no right to coerce. Again let me emphasize that I am asking merely whether any plausible political theories might differentiate between insiders and outsiders. Whether such a theory is ultimately valid is a question for domestic political theory.

The Entanglement of Benefits and Coercion

These two rudimentary explanations for how affirmative obligations might be limited to those subject to state coercion stem from the fact that the state's right to coerce an individual might ultimately be an important element in the rationale for requiring affirmative assistance. There is reason to think that there may be other ways to argue that benefits can be limited to those who are subject to coercion. Entitlements to benefits and subjection to coercion, speaking generally, are tightly entangled. Extending the right to benefits beyond the state's coercive powers is problematic both because it is sometimes unclear what counts as a benefit as opposed to coercion and because benefits, once bestowed, may justify extending the state's coercive powers.

DISTINGUISHING BENEFITS FROM BURDENS

The argument in favor of affirmative assistance seems to address only the extension of benefits and to assume that it will be possible uncontroversially to identify benefits as those things that the recipients themselves actually want. Extending benefits to outsiders will then amount to treating them equally. The problem with this simple assumption is that the only thing that differentiates equal treatment from intervention, and discrimination from respect for another state's sovereignty, is whether the treatment in question is perceived as a benefit by the recipient.

Assume, for instance, that one nation sets out to provide another with medical assistance. Since birth-control devices and abortion are both legally and culturally acceptable in the donor state, they are offered to the recipient state as part of the total package of medical aid. Doctors sent into the state will make those services available along with everything else. If the recipient favors provision of birth control and abortion, then extending these benefits will be approved as equal treatment and refusal to extend them would be thought discriminatory. If the recipient state disapproves abortion and contraception, then any efforts by the donor state to make them available will be disapproved as interventionist; in contrast, the donor's forbidding the doctors to dispense such services would constitute respect for sovereignty.

The only way that the donor state can satisfy both the norm of nonintervention and the norm of nondiscrimination would be to allow the recipient state and the individual recipients the choice of whether the services should be allowed. If the donor state simply extends all of the services to those in other nations, it acts in a nondiscriminatory manner but risks intervening beyond its legitimate scope of authority if the recipient state prefers that the services not be provided. If the donor state treats individuals differently because they are outside its scope of authority and if the recipient state prefers that services be rendered, the donor is discriminating.

This problem arises in a particularly acute manner in the context of extraterritorial application of legal rules and institutions. Of current importance is the question whether the United States should regulate the activities of its multinational corporations in other countries. If a multinational injures someone in another state, should the generous American rules be applied to allow recovery?[7] On the one hand, refusal to extend the benefits of American law is discriminatory because foreigners are denied the benefits allowed to persons injured in the United States. On the other hand, it is presumptuous of the United States to seek to regulate activities occurring elsewhere in the world, as if its law was superior to that of other countries.

The only sure way to avoid such criticism is to allow the other state or the foreigner to determine on a case-by-case basis when U.S. law would apply and when it would not. By exercising such control, the other state could denominate which exercises of U.S. power it found offensively interventionist and which it found properly nondiscriminatory. It could say, for instance, that U.S. law ought not to dictate the method of carrying out business within the country but that if an injury was caused by conduct legal under local law, then the more restrictive American standard of conduct should be applied to determine whether recovery was permissible. By allowing other states to evaluate the relevance of U.S. law case by case, the United States would forestall any criticism by the other country that application of U.S. law was interventionist or that failure of application was discriminatory.

The problem with this suggestion is surely plain. The other state is allowed all of the benefits but none of the burdens of U.S. law. As a corollary, the American acting abroad is allowed none of the benefits but all of the burdens. In short, this suggestion amounts to limiting the coercive reach of local institutions but taking the most expansive view of affirmative duties. This is a safe strategy if one's goal is always to make outsiders happy but seems both unnecessarily generous to those outside the state's coercive reach and unduly harsh on citizens.

Another alternative that has been suggested in the literature looks like a compromise but may actually incorporate the worst of both

[7]Shue, "Exporting Hazards."

worlds. One might formulate a special norm to apply to interjurisdictional situations. U.S. corporations, for instance, have subsidiaries in
Mexico that engage in asbestos manufacturing methods that would be
illegal in the United States because they are unduly hazardous to
workers. Should American regulations be applied to injuries suffered
in Mexico? The dilemma, of course, is that refusal to apply U.S. law
is discriminatory, but applying it seems paternalistic. The suggested
solution is an informed consent rule whereby Mexican workers would
be informed of the special dangers and allowed to make up their own
minds.[8]

There are two serious problems with such a solution. The first is
that it creates a whole new set of threshold issues. When is the activity
sufficiently American to make the "real" American law apply, as
opposed to the watered down, informed consent version? What if an
American worker for an American company is injured on the job in
Mexico? What if half of her years of employment in the company
were at the Mexican plant of the American company? And so forth.
Instead of a single problematic boundary between U.S. and Mexican
law, there must now be a boundary between Mexican law and the
special interjurisdictional norm and a boundary between the special
norm and U.S. domestic law. The difficulty, in other words, is to
differentiate between purely domestic vertical relations and diagonal
ones.

Second, none of the problems of discrimination and paternalism
have been solved. U.S. law still has problematic, paternalistic effects
in Mexico, because its existence gave rise to the special norm.
Moreover, the worker who is injured in Mexico can still complain
about being treated differently from a comparable person injured in
the United States. American workers, after all, are protected by a
blanket prohibition against hazards in the workplace. Why should
Mexican workers have to make the difficult individual choice of
either consenting to hazardous conditions or going without a job?
And it is neither more nor less convincing to explain the different
treatment in terms of boundaries and of differences in local law than it
would have been to offer the same explanation for applying Mexican
domestic law in the first place.

---

[8]Shue, "Exporting Hazards."

Admittedly, most arguments for affirmative assistance do not involve such ambiguous "benefits" as birth control or legal norms. Famine-relief aid would seem to be an unqualified good (although one finds occasional examples where a government restricts provision of such aid because the aid would benefit groups that the government is attempting to suppress). In such situations the ambiguity argument has little if any force. Unambiguous cases do not undercut the point in less straightforward cases, however. For one state to meet obligations of both affirmative assistance and nonintervention, it must allow the recipient state to choose what it considers beneficial. As soon as it imposes its own definition of benefits, it exercises coercive power beyond its legitimate scope of authority.

BENEFITS AND EXTENSION OF COERCIVE POWERS

The second way in which coercion, generally, is entangled with benefits is that the provision of benefits arguably gives a reason to extend coercion more broadly. The scope of coercion seems to "catch up" with the scope of benefits.

Assume, for example, that the donor country has supplied a recipient country with food, medical, and agricultural aid. It now claims that its action imposes on the recipients of such aid an obligation to support its political agenda. Since the donations came from a capitalist system (say) that is effective at producing goods, the recipient state must adopt a capitalist system also. Furthermore, it must support the donor's foreign-policy objectives. Recognizing that the benefits conferred are not as extensive as those that its own citizens receive, the donor does not seek to impose a full range of political obligations. It nonetheless asserts a lesser degree of political obligation, commensurate with the benefits received. Is this argument convincing as a matter of political theory?

Let us first differentiate this argument from two similar ones that we addressed earlier. First, it is different from the quid-pro-quo argument about limiting obligations of affirmative assistance. That argument took as fixed and given the limits of a state's coercive power and asked whether it might be defensible to limit the right to benefits accordingly. Here we assume that benefits are being given and we ask whether obligations might fluctuate accordingly. In a sense, then, our present argument more nearly resembles the benefits theory of political obligation. It resembles the "fair play" theory that a state's right to coerce is founded on provisions of benefits created by a common cooperative enterprise.

The present argument is also different from the benefits theory. Earlier we said that a state could not initially base its claim to coerce individuals on a benefits theory because the theory presumed that sovereignty had already been shown. Unless sovereignty has already been shown, the state has no claim to withhold or distribute benefits. This objection is not germane in the present context; we do not need to justify sovereignty as an initial matter because at this point in the argument sovereignty presumably has been shown. We start with an assumption of sovereignty over particular territory, assets, and people and then argue that when benefits are extended to outsiders, obligations go along with them. So long as the state is already presumed to have established its sovereignty over what it is distributing, the argument is not circular or question begging.

One suspects that this argument would surprise some of the political theorists who have asserted that there is an obligation of international affirmative assistance. They argue that the donor owes something to the recipient, but they do not then go on to argue that the recipient has political obligations in return.[9] Yet if one finds the benefits theory plausible, then one ought to address the question of its force in this context. If obligations can be grounded on benefits domestically, why not also internationally? All of this adds to the general puzzle of extending benefits beyond the legitimate scope of coercion. Obviously the two are tightly entangled, and although there may ultimately be ways to assign benefits a broader scope than coercion, there also seem to be plausible reasons to assign them the *same* scope.

[9]Perhaps the claim will be made that if the donor *owes* assistance to the foreign recipient, then the receipt of benefits cannot function as a basis for obligation. The problem with making this argument in the international context is the same as with making it in the domestic context. In the domestic context, one might also argue that benefits cannot be a basis for obligation because the state has obligations of affirmative assistance. Yet it would seem that the state most deserving of political support would be the one that concentrates on providing the essential needs of its citizens, precisely the ones it is most likely to "owe." Support is due, in other words, precisely because one's state fulfills its responsibilities.

The Apparent Assymetry of Negative
and Positive Rights

The irony of this conclusion—that the vertical thesis might permit denying to noncitizens benefits that are extended to citizens—is that it is precisely in the literature arguing for affirmative international obligations that domestic political theory has had its most pronounced international impact. The domestic theory that has been applied to the problem of international obligations to assist is that of John Rawls in *A Theory of Justice*. There is considerable debate in the literature over whether, contrary to Rawls's original suggestion, redistribution ought to take place across national boundaries.[10] What seems striking for present purposes is the apparently close connection between the vertical argument that political theory is applicable to diagonal relationships and the conclusion in the literature that domestic theories of redistribution apply in international situations. To certain authors, at least, it has seemed intuitively clear that when one applies domestic theories internationally, citizens and noncitizens should be entitled to the same affirmative rights.

There is a clash between the intuition of equality and the conclusion that affirmative aid may be withheld from noncitizens under certain plausible domestic political theories. The intuitions clash in that, on the one hand, the very essence of the vertical thesis is that diagonal relations are not qualitatively different from domestic vertical ones and, on the other, we have suggested that it is not necessarily required that affirmative rights be extended, as negative rights are, to those beyond the state's coercive power. Both intuitions seem plausible on their face yet are seen to be inconsistent once compared. Why, under our vertical analysis, are negative rights different from positive rights?

The answer is that they are not so different. The vertical thesis holds that the same standard should be applied to assess the legit-

---

[10]For discussions of whether Rawls's arguments about redistribution apply internationally, see Beitz, *Political Theory*; Peter Danielson, "Theories, Intuitions, and the Problem of Worldwide Distributive Justice," *Philosophy of Social Sciences* 3 (1973): 331–40; David Richards, "International Distributive Justice," in Pennock and Chapman, *Ethics, Economics, and the Law*; Thomas Pogge, *Realizing Rawls* (forthcoming from Cornell University Press).

imacy of all of the state's activities, whether diagonal or purely domestic. The fact that the same standard is applied does not mean that identical treatment will result. Indeed, in the context of negative rights, it is quite clear that identical treatment will *not* result. Frequently, citizens will be subject to coercion where noncitizens would not be. The same standard for whether coercion is legitimate, when evenhandedly applied, will in the general course of things make coercion of the citizen more justifiable; a single standard requires different treatment. The equality of treatment that the vertical thesis requires operates to establish a general standard of legitimacy of state action. For the same reason, the vertical thesis requires that a theory of affirmative assistance or redistribution should be phrased so as to apply to diagonal and purely domestic vertical relationships equally. The standard itself may treat the two cases differently if there is some appropriate factor distinguishing the two. The factor that might arguably be appropriate is whether the would-be recipient is subject to state coercion.

The reason that several authors have concluded that there should be equal access to affirmative benefits may have to do with the fact that redistribution is considered in relative isolation from a general vertical appraisal of international theory. A general vertical analysis of international relations makes the legitimacy of coercion an appropriate topic for political analysis. If one keeps in mind the difference between citizens and noncitizens in terms of their obligations to support the state, then it does not seem nearly so odd that there might be differences in terms of their rights to affirmative assistance as well. The comparison to a state's right to coerce makes it clear that applying political theory evenhandedly is not the same as requiring equal treatment. On first appearance, a theory of affirmative assistance that gives the same rights to benefits to *everyone*, simply because they are human beings, is appealing. But in the context of a general vertical appraisal of international relations, the treatment of coercion stands as a reminder that political rights may be unevenly distributed throughout the population even by a theory that applies equally to everyone.

Considering these issues together also makes differentiation between citizens and noncitizens more plausible because the differentiation may be based on the fact that the former are more subject to coercion than the latter. An individual's right to be left alone is prior to the right to assistance in the following sense. Political theory first applies to all individuals equally, to determine who is subject to state coercion. This first step of the analysis separates individuals into two groups, namely, those subject to coercion and those not subject to it. At the next step, application of the rationale of affirmative assistance may have a different impact on the two groups, because the difference between the groups may be relevant to the second question. The answer to the first question in this way affects the resolution of the second. Affirmative rights are distributed unevenly because they are distributed only once negative rights are distributed; but this raises the question why the two sorts of rights are not distributed in the opposite order.

The question of the state's right to coerce has priority because the state has nothing to distribute until its right to coerce has been demonstrated. From what source is it supposed to obtain assets to distribute? Its sovereignty must first be established, either direct sovereignty over resources or some right of taxation. There can be no duty to assist, in other words, without means of assistance, and therefore the question of the state's right to govern versus the individual's right to be left alone must have been settled already.

Other Bases for International Duties

Persons seeking to present the strongest possible case for affirmative international duties might be more successful if they relied on some foundation other than the argument that duties to citizens are equally applicable to noncitizens. There are several other strategies for arguing in favor of international assistance.

One strategy is to return to the earlier argument that political theory requires a justification for national boundaries. I examined this argument in the context of the state's right to coerce, an issue of negative liberty. Once the state has justified sovereignty over its territory, the arbitrariness of state borders does not provide a foundation for the argument in favor of international redistribution. However, if the question has not successfully been answered in the context of negative liberty, then there is also no answer to the question in the context of affirmative international duties. Therefore, the best strategy for establishing affirmative duties may be to undercut state sovereignty over territory or natural resources for both purposes at once.

This strategy may have appeal to those persons who have argued that the arbitrariness of borders supports a duty of international assistance. The costs of relying on this strategy should be considered carefully, however, for the argument that because borders are arbitrary the state's territorial sovereignty is unproven leads to extreme conclusions. It does much more than merely entitle necessitous noncitizens to a share of the state's assets. It also immunizes citizens to demands that they support their own state. If they have no such obligations, they cannot be compelled to make sacrifices to aid the international redistribution. Furthermore, in a sense this argument is not about redistribution at all. The essence of the argument is that the state is not now properly sovereign over its territory or assets. The conclusion is not that the state must redistribute assets but that present claims of sovereignty are fraudulent. Moreover, whether outsiders could appropriate the state's assets would not depend on whether they were necessitous.

The strategy therefore leads one toward both anarchism and extreme cosmopolitanism. The way to stop short of these apparent logical conclusions is not obvious. One would need to argue that there is adequate sovereignty both to coerce citizens and to rebuf the claims of nonnecessitous outsiders, but not enough to override the claims of necessitous outsiders.

Other possible strategies for arguing in favor of international assistance rely on familiar horizontal reasoning. The first is whether there might be a horizontal relationship between states such that assistance is owed. Focusing on vertical relationships does not deny the possibility of such horizontal obligations between states. Indeed, the remedial argument that affirmative assistance corrects past injustices and the contractual argument that it fulfills earlier promises are typically horizontal arguments of this sort.

The second—and it should not be underestimated—is that there may be horizontal relations between individual people. To say that a state, qua state, has no *political* obligation to help those whom it may not coerce in no way denies the existence of a moral responsibility of affluent persons to help other persons in need. This argument of horizontal equity arises independently of, and in addition to, whatever vertical relations might be thought to exist. Moral philosophers have struggled with this difficult problem; it is certainly not irrelevant simply because it remains unsolved. Nor is it irrelevant simply because vertical political relations imposing affirmative obligations do not necessarily exist.

Chapter Seven

Humanitarian Intervention

Religious oppression, totalitarianism, and political imprisonment have always been concerns of political theory, and in the twentieth century they have also become concerns of international law. With our growing awareness of events in distant places, we are increasingly confronted with the dilemma of whether we should try to do anything about them. If a government is systematically violating the rights of its citizens, should other nations intervene?[1] This question is at the intersection of the two issues just discussed, intervention and affirmative assistance. We ask whether one state *may* intervene on humanitarian grounds; with regard to affirmative assistance, we ask whether it *must* intervene.

Redefining the Problem

For present purposes, I will define humanitarian intervention precisely but somewhat narrowly. First, I assume that the violator of

[1]There is an extensive literature on the subject. The commentary runs from Hugo Grotious, *De jure belli est pacis*, chap. 25, and Emer Vattel, *Le droit des gens*, chap. 4, sec. 56 up through the present, for example, Richard Lillich, "Intervention to Protect Human Rights," *McGill Law Journal* 15 (June 1969): 205.

rights is a recognized governmental entity such as a nation state. I differentiate such an entity from terrorist organizations, rebel movements that have not achieved governmental status, and purely private persons. I likewise assume that the entity seeking to intervene is a recognized governmental entity and not a private party.

Second, I assume that the violations complained about are in fact politically illegitimate, that the governmental entity committing them can offer no valid political justification for the violations as a matter of domestic theory. Typically, the activities in question violate human rights. Human-rights violations cannot be authorized by a valid political theory because to say that the rights violated are natural human rights is to say that they are protected from government abuse. I set aside, therefore, the difficult problems of defining what rights exist and determining whether they have been violated. Obviously, there are important controversies over such issues. For example, it might be argued that women's rights are culturally specific, that they do not exist—or they take a radically different form—in societies where women are the property of their fathers or husbands. Without addressing the validity of such claims of cultural specificity, this discussion assumes for purposes of argument that the rights asserted as a basis for humanitarian intervention indeed exist and are violated in the case in question. This presumption is in keeping with a focus on the implications of a vertical analysis, as a general matter, rather than on the implications of any particular political theory.

The presumption that rights are indeed being violated may or may not entail the fact that the rights holders themselves favor outside intervention on their behalf. As a matter of domestic theory, one might believe that individuals are entitled to waive their rights or to prefer to live with the violations rather than seek outside assistance. Or one might adhere to a more paternalistic theory of rights and maintain that even if people do not want their rights they can be forced to have them anyway. Perhaps, after all, the rights holders have been brainwashed into accepting the existing violations. In accordance with our general agnosticism about particular political theories, we need not make assumptions here about whether the rights holders favor intervention; we make only the weaker assumption that their rights are being violated. If an individualistic theory of rights allows persons to waive rights, then under such a theory (but only under such a theory) would a desire for outside intervention be required.

Third, I limit the discussion to cases in which the intervening state is acting out of pure humanitarian motives. The state does not selectively intervene in the affairs of only those states that it dislikes for political reasons, nor does it attempt to use rights violations as an excuse for meddling in activities that do not involve rights violations. This definition of the problem does not necessarily require that the state intervene in every violation; arguably, it may reserve its assistance for cases where it expects to be effective, or perhaps cases where intervention will not be too costly. What will not count as humanitarian intervention for present purposes, however, is a politically motivated decision to intervene, even in situations where human-rights violations do exist.

Why should we define the problem so narrowly? Hemmed in by so many definitional restrictions, we perhaps shall not find any true cases of humanitarian intervention. The motivation is analytical simplification. Departing from any of the conditions makes the problem more difficult than it would otherwise be. Pure cases of humanitarian intervention are difficult enough to address, without admitting additional complications. I am not claiming that an action cannot be considered humanitarian simply because the government has mixed humanitarian and political motives, or that the intervention is for that reason illegitimate. The point is simply that one can bracket such questions, reserving them until one understands better the purer instances of the problem. This chapter attempts only a preliminary investigation of the problem of humanitarian intervention to the extent that it does not address any of these complications.

It simplifies, also, in another way. At the outset, we take for purposes of critical investigation a somewhat exaggerated statement of the position against humanitarian intervention. That extreme position against humanitarian intervention holds that intervention is never justified by the fact that a government is committing human-rights violations, no matter how clear and egregious the violations are and no matter how carefully the intervening state attempts to limit itself to remedying the rights violations. This position is an application of the principle of state autonomy discussed earlier.

It is extreme in that it makes no exceptions for even truly outrageous violations and in that few people would hold such a view. Despite the rhetoric of state autonomy, and the willingness of some authors to apply that rhetoric to certain situations in which human rights are violated,[2] how many of us feel it correct to look the other way at genocide, as in the case of Nazi Germany? At apartheid? At Idi Amin's Uganda? Nonetheless, it is worthwhile to take the extreme argument at face value and try to understand what moral logic it might draw on. To the extent that moderate opponents of humanitarian intervention might compromise between respect for human rights and the traditional values of state autonomy, it is worthwhile to evaluate the normative status of the principles they compromise. And if we find ourselves rejecting the extreme position, our understanding of why we do so will help us formulate a more moderate position. To understand *why* humanitarian intervention is sometimes allowable is to understand something about *when* it is allowable.

For these reasons, we start with a clarification of the hypothesis that one state may never intervene in the domestic affairs of another in order to prevent human-rights violations. The extreme position that humanitarian intervention is never appropriate might at first seem to be merely the consistent application of a particular domestic political theory. Nation states might be thought justified by a purely territorial account of political theory; within their territories, they reign supreme. Any actions committed within their territories are justifiable, but states are not entitled to act outside those territories. This particular political theory would generate something resembling the extreme position on humanitarian intervention. It would justify whatever domestic actions a state might take and make humanitarian intervention unavailable by denying the existence of substantive rights against the state. It would also prohibit other states from intervening on the grounds that outside their own territories they would have no justification for acting.

There are several necessary modifications of this interpretation of the argument against humanitarian intervention. First, it is not entirely clear whether the prohibition on humanitarian intervention

---

[2]For an argument that the intervention by Tanzania into Idi Amin's Uganda was an illegitimate violation of Ugandan sovereignty, see Farooq Hassan, "Realpolitik in International Law: After Tanzanian-Uganda Conflict, 'Humanitarian Intervention' Reexamined," *Willamette Law Review* 17 (Fall 1981): 859.

operates territorially. What if a state violates the rights of its own citizens, but it does so while they are present in another state (for instance, its secret police track down and murder citizens while they are abroad)? It is arguable that a prohibition on humanitarian intervention (if one exists) might also apply to this type of state action. Conversely, it is possible that the prohibition would not apply to violations of the rights of noncitizens that are temporarily present within the territory when their rights are violated. The scope of state autonomy, in other words, might be defined in other than territorial terms. It is possible that state autonomy is instead defined in terms of the state's control over its own citizens.

Assume then that freedom from humanitarian intervention might be defined either in territorial terms or in terms of control over a particular group of individuals. This analysis still does not really account, however, for the position that humanitarian intervention is inappropriate. The basic problem is that it relies on an assumption that *there can be* no domestic human-rights violations. The state has complete authority within its own territory or over its own citizens; if this is true, then it is justified in every domestic action that it takes. There are simply no substantive limitations protecting human rights within the constituting political theory.

In contrast, the more usual position against humanitarian intervention does not necessarily deny that domestic human-rights violations can occur. Instead, it suggests that even if there are human-rights violations, they are not an adequate basis for intervention by other nations. Persons believing that humanitarian intervention is always inappropriate may nonetheless believe that local persons are treated unjustly by their own state and have a domestic right to rebel. This belief is inconsistent with the assumption that, within its own territory, the state is entitled to do what it pleases.

There are various strategic reasons why opponents of humanitarian intervention might not simply deny that rights exist. Above all they may find that the position is philosophically implausible or politically untenable. No modern state would want to have to defend itself against intervention by claiming complete and totalitarian authority over the lives and liberties of its citizens. Such a claim almost seems an admission that the state is totalitarian. A state would rather deny that there are rights violations but also claim that no other state has the right to second guess this assessment. This stance is both philosophically more plausible and strategically preferable.

The argument against humanitarian intervention is thus best understood not as a denial of any right but as a denial of any international remedy. The argument is that while as a theoretical matter a state may sometimes violate the rights of its own people or commit violations within its own territory, the only remedy is a domestic and not an international one. Citizens may resist (if indeed a violation exists), but other nations are not permitted to help them.[3] This is the claim that we must investigate. The argument in favor of humanitarian intervention defines the problem favorably to claims for intervention: at issue is an admitted human-rights or political-rights violation, perpetrated by a government, and opposed by another government that is sincerely motivated and not merely out for political gain. Aligned against this position is the response that while a violation of rights may exist, international intervention is the wrong remedy. How do these arguments fare under a vertical analysis?

Permissibility of Humanitarian Intervention

A horizontal analysis of humanitarian intervention would focus on the relationship between the state that is violating political or human rights and the state that seeks to intervene. A vertical analysis, in contrast, identifies and analyzes the relationships between states and the individuals subject to their influence. At least three vertical relations are of potential relevance to a vertical appraisal of humanitarian intervention. The first is the relationship between the violating state and its victim; it arguably gives rise to a claim that this political relationship deserves protection from outside interference. The second is the relationship between the intervening state and the perpetrator of the rights violation; it arguably gives rise to a claim that the intervenor has exceeded the scope of its legitimate authority. The third is the relationship between the intervenor and the victim; it

---

[3]This, more or less, is Michael Walzer's position, although he carefully qualifies it so that the presumption may be rebutted in appropriate cases. ''The Moral Standing of States: A Response to Four Critics,'' *Philosophy and Public Affairs* 9 (Summer 1980).

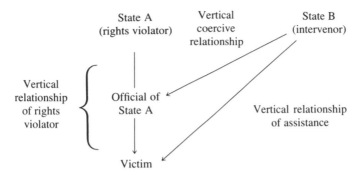

Figure 5. Vertical relations and humanitarian intervention

arguably gives rise to a claim that the intervenor has an obligation to assist (see Figure 5).

The force of the first vertical argument (if accepted) would be to shield the violator-victim relationship from interference. If the second sort of relationship is acknowledged, this would establish a right to intervene. We shall see, however, that neither of these vertical arguments is easy to make. The third would also establish a right (indeed, an obligation) to intervene; but again, such a relationship may be hard to establish. We will examine below how the nature of particular constituting political theories would influence the recognition of political relationships of these three types. The usual argument disallowing humanitarian intervention is roughly equivalent to denying all three. In other words, while it denies that the relationship between the violator and the victim warrants affirmative theoretical protection, it also denies that the appropriate remedy is intervention by another state. To argue in favor of humanitarian intervention, one must deny protection to the first political relationship but establish the legitimacy of either the second or the third.

THE VIOLATOR-VICTIM RELATIONSHIP

The argument based on the first of these vertical relationships seems unsound. Since the victim is within the scope of the violating state's authority, it is argued, this vertical relationship is somehow protected from outside intervention. Authority to regulate must mean authority to regulate free from outside interference. The power to regulate, so the argument goes, would not amount to much if it did not create a corresponding prohibition against others' interfering with the exercise of that power.

In response, one might argue, first, that where there are violations of substantive human rights, there can be no authority to regulate, and so a protected relationship simply does not exist. We started, after all, by assuming for purposes of argument that rights are being violated. Yet this response may be too simple. Although a state may be exceeding its scope of legitimate authority by violating human rights, this violation does not automatically terminate the political relationship because a protected relationship may still exist even if the state abuses it. South Africa may violate the rights of its black citizens, but the violation does not entirely break the tie that binds them, even though it may give them just cause to refuse to obey. The question is whether a relationship that concededly exists must be protected from outside intervention even though it is abused.

Other objections, however, more convincingly support the conclusion that illegitimate political relationships should not be insulated from outside interference. As a matter of domestic theory, the illegitimacy may give the victim a right to resist; similarly, the victim might be thought entitled to enlist the support of fellow citizens in defense of his or her rights through a domestic resistance movement. The conditions under which such a response is appropriate are, of course, an issue of domestic political theory. From a vertical perspective then, the relevant question is whether there is any principled reason to differentiate between formation of a domestic resistance movement and acceptance of assistance from abroad.

If there are any such reasons to differentiate, they arise not from the sanctity of the victim-violator relationship but from the external status of the intervenor. The status of the outside intervenor would seem to have no relevance to the protected status of the victim-violator relationship. The vertical relationship between the victim and the violating state cannot account for any presumption against humanitarian interference. That relationship is not insulated from outside intervention per se, for if it is protected at all, it is at most protected from intervention by *other state actors*. The right to regulate does not of itself place obligations on others not to interfere with regulation, even if that right is abused; for in some cases interference with an abused right to regulate is permissible.

Under a vertical perspective, therefore, the most important domestic question is whether the applicable political theories treat political relationships as so deserving of protection that they might not be upset by third parties of any kind. If so, then they would protect against intervention by other states. As we have just seen, some political theories might conceivably do so, but they need not. A political theory might provide that the victim has a right to resist but that no one has a right to assist him or her, not even a domestic resistance movement. Or a political theory might hold that even the victim is not entitled to resist. If the pertinent political justifications do, however, recognize (as most plausible theories probably do) that third parties may help human-rights victims resist, the next question would be whether there was any principled reason for limiting such assistance to sources within the same nation. If outside governments are prohibited from intervening, the reason for the prohibition cannot be the sanctity of the political relationship but must instead be a tenet that interference may not come *from other states*. The explanation for the presumption against humanitarian interference, in other words, is a product of some limitations on the interfering state.

The horizontal perspective holds as much; the acting state is limited in its relationships with other states. And a horizontal account of the presumption against humanitarian intervention does indeed focus on the identity of the intervening actor. However, the identity of the would-be intervenor is not relevant to an explanation relying on the nature of the relationship between violator and victim. This first vertical relationship—the violator-victim relationship—thus seems unlikely under most political theories to prohibit humanitarian intervention.

The focus of the inquiry thus turns from the supposed sanctity of the first relationship, that between the individual victim and the violating state, to the second, that between the intervening state and those individuals in the violator state who are responsible for the violations. The focus shifts, in other words, to the question whether the intervening state's exercise of coercive power outside its own territory and against a noncitizen can be justified in terms of its constituting political theory when the purpose of the coercive action is to prevent or punish human-rights violations.

Under a vertical approach, a more serious basis for a presumption against humanitarian intervention may be that the intervening state simply lacks the authority to act. Typically, the human-rights violations in question are committed by noncitizens of the intervening state and are committed outside the state; where is the basis for coercion? By hypothesis, we seem to be dealing with a situation in which, were it not for the rights violations, there would be no authority for the state to formulate or enforce its norms of positive law. A question thus arises whether the fact that the violation is one of natural human rights rather than positive-law norms gives the intervening state a legitimate claim to act.

Because the intervening state is simply enforcing protections stemming from political theory and not formulating them in the first instance, the issue is (to use legal terms) not one of jurisdiction to legislate but one of jurisdiction to enforce. The state is seeking to compel adherence to human-rights norms that exist independently and that already apply, in the abstract, to the conduct in question. In this sense, the matter resembles the international law principle of "universal" jurisdiction. It was thought that some crimes were so outrageous that they were subject to punishment by any state that caught the offenders, regardless of where the crime occurred. Piracy was an example.[4]

Does the fact that a certain action violated universal norms of human rights give any state whatsoever the right to prevent or punish it, even in situations where the enforcing state would have no right to apply its own positive law? Or is enforcement limited to states that would also have the authority to apply their own positive law? Answers depend on domestic political theory as well as on the international law of humanitarian intervention because the questions concern the foundation of coercive authority. The issue is whether it is an

[4]A.L.I. Restatement (Revised) of Foreign Relations Law sec. 404. (1987).

adequate theoretical basis for coercion that the coercion prevents or punishes a violation of natural law.

Admittedly, as a domestic matter, we are more accustomed to discussions of whether consistency with natural law is a *necessary* condition for political legitimacy than to discussions of whether it is a *sufficient* condition. A common subject is whether there exist obligations to support an unjust regime or obey an unjust law. Should one support positive law that is repugnant to natural law? Here the question concerns the status of natural law that is not at the same time positive law rather than positive law that is not at the same time consistent with natural law.

For this reason, the problem of humanitarian intervention resembles not the classic problems of civil disobedience but rather the issue of the legitimacy of the postwar trials of Nazi war criminals. If extermination of Jews was permissible under the positive law in force at the time, is it fair to apply norms of natural law "retroactively"? In the Nuremberg trials, the governments that were prosecuting Nazi officials would have had no right to apply at trial pure norms of positive law to what had gone on in Germany during the Nazi period; did the natural law status of the norms they were enforcing give them a right to assert coercive authority?

Although in the actual Nuremberg case enforcement was at the hands of other nations, a similar problem can arise purely domestically. For instance, if a democratic regime takes over after a dictatorship, it may face the problem whether to punish human-rights violators from previous regimes. Unless, perhaps, in particular cases it were possible to argue that they had violated the positive law of the period as well as human rights, the argument for punishing them would be based on their offenses against natural law. This is a temporal variant of the general issue, of which humanitarian intervention is the spatial counterpart, namely, whether natural law unaccompanied by any positive authority is an adequate basis for coercion. Can a later government, or one spatially removed, punish human-rights violations?

Obviously, there are arguments both ways. On the one hand, one might think that natural law is in itself an adequate basis for coercion, even when positive authority is absent. In formulating positive laws, so the argument might go, it is important to allow the affected individuals input into the decision-making process because the decision might permissibly be made either way. Process rights are therefore important in positive law; and the applicability of positive law should be limited to those persons who have a right to assist in its choice or formulation. However, natural law norms are not chosen in this sense; they exist independently. Thus, according to this argument, the limitations that one would place on the range of positive law are not relevant to natural law.

From the contrary perspective, the decision to enforce a law and the process of enforcing it are themselves political acts. The identity of those enforcing the law is therefore crucial, even when natural-law norms are involved. In American law, for example, the right to be tried by a properly chosen judge and jury is as important a procedural right in a case of murder as in a technical antitrust violation. Maybe even more important. Even if murder is an offense against natural law, there may still be important reasons to limit enforcement of that natural law to (for example) a jury of one's peers. There is a process right, in other words, even where the underlying norm is based on natural law, so that the governmental body exercising coercive authority must be one that has proper authority over the violator's person.

This argument that enforcement must come at the hands of an entity with legitimate sovereign authority would be one argument on which a presumption against humanitarian intervention might rest. Others could probably be formulated to support the same conclusion. The conclusion is that the government that seeks to intervene simply has no right to take remedial action just because there has been a violation of natural human rights. Unless the state has the sort of authority over the individuals that would suffice for legitimate application of its positive law, it simply lacks the necessary right to act. The vertical perspective does not indicate whether this argument should ultimately be accepted or rejected. It simply searches for domestic analogies to the international problem at issue, such as trials of human-rights violators from past regimes, and asserts that one's reactions to such domestic problems are appropriate guides for one's solution to the international analogs.

THE INTERVENOR-VICTIM RELATIONSHIP

What seems to be missing in the analogy between retroactive punishment and humanitarian intervention is that in the former the harm has already been done whereas in the latter there is still some possibility of correcting the abuses. Preventing further abuses is the primary motivation behind arguments for intervention. The fact that this aspect is not reflected in our analysis of the intervenor-perpetrator relationship does not mean that our analysis of the relationship is faulty. Instead, it means that there is an additional vertical relationship that remains to be considered, namely, the link between the intervening state and the victim. This link does not appear in most cases where mere retroactive punishment is sought. Instead, it arises in situations where the victims request prospective help in preventing future violations. It is the third vertical relationship of potential relevance to an evaluation of humanitarian intervention.

The question of humanitarian intervention is usually phrased in terms of whether one state *may* intervene in another's domestic affairs in order to prevent human-rights violations. However, there is also a question whether a state *has an obligation* to intervene. The first is a question of negative liberty, the second one of affirmative assistance. For example, it is arguable that Americans and Europeans had an obligation to attempt to compel the Nazis to change their policies of extermination even before World War II; that we have a responsibility to undertake our best efforts to force South Africa to abandon apartheid; or that we ought to admit asylum seekers and use our influence to force other nations to allow free emigration. If such obligations exist, it is possible that they might provide an answer to the question just discussed, namely, the legitimacy of the intervenor-perpetrator relationship. The right to intervene would arguably stem from an affirmative obligation to help the victims.

The earlier discussion of affirmative duties is relevant here. Whether a state has an obligation to help those beyond its borders is a function of whether a state's political theory recognizes affirmative duties domestically and whether the reasons for this domestic recognition extend to the international situation. If affirmative duties are owed simply on the basis of common humanity, then outsiders may be as entitled to assistance as insiders. But some bases for affirmative duties might differentiate between those subject to a state's authority and those not subject, as where assistance is a quid pro quo for supporting the government. The first question, therefore, is whether an affirmative duty of assistance even exists.

A straightforward application of our earlier reasoning about affirmative assistance will not suffice, however. Humanitarian intervention has an added complication, the element of coercion. Horizontally, there is another state involved, which is resisting the assistance. Vertically, the individuals who are causing the violation must be coerced if the violations are to be stopped. The question is, therefore, whether this added element changes the calculations of whether affirmative assistance is due. Or, to put it another way, where both nonintervention and assistance are potentially implicated in a human-rights violation, what effect do the two issues have on each other? If a state would otherwise lack a basis for coercing the violator, then does an affirmative obligation to the victim create one?

Let us try to imagine a situation in which such an argument might be made. Assume that the United States treats civil liberties as something to which citizens are affirmatively entitled. It is not just that the government is not supposed to violate citizens' civil liberties; it must (under the hypothesized constituting political theory) take any positive steps necessary to assure the enjoyment of them. Furthermore, assume that the foundation for this duty to assist lies in the rights that people have as human beings rather than in anything special about the relationship between citizens and their own government. This obligation of affirmative assistance therefore applies to noncitizens as well as to citizens, and the United States (under this theory) therefore has obligations to help protect outsiders from political persecution. Assume further that in its desire to comply with this duty in the international arena, the United States runs up against a competing principle prohibiting coercion of persons not subject to its positive legal authority. As a general matter, its constituting political theory does not give a right to enforce natural law without a foundation in positive authority.

If the obligation to assist can itself provide a basis for coercive intervention, certain sorts of efforts to enforce natural law would nonetheless be arguably justifiable. It would be more justifiable to intervene where there existed an affirmative duty to assist than where no such prospective remedial purpose existed. Intervention to prevent the occurrence of human-rights violations, or to discontinue existing ones, would be on a stronger foundation than punishment after the fact for violations that have already occurred. Intuitively, this seems a sensible conclusion. It leads one to wonder whether our sentiments favoring humanitarian intervention might not be founded more strongly on an obligation to assist innocent victims beyond our borders than on any right to enforce natural law. It is not the intervening state's vertical relationship with the violator that gives it a right to intervene on humanitarian grounds but its vertical relationship with the victim.

Yet to accept this interpretation of the right of humanitarian intervention leads to a rather stringent set of practical limitations on its exercise. Indeed, in actual problems somewhat comparable to our hypothetical one, the United States will very likely be unable to meet the conditions for intervention. Under what circumstances might the United States justify intervention on the grounds of a *duty* to protect civil liberties abroad? First, to overcome a presumption against coercion of the violators, there must actually be an affirmative duty of the sort described. This condition was assumed to be met in our hypothetical case, but seems less plausible in the real world. In the civil liberty context, it is not even clear that an affirmative duty can be shown domestically. Our constituting theory provides certain civil liberties, but they may all be negative liberties, such that the state might meet its burden through inaction. If our tradition of civil liberties means only that our government may not affirmatively violate them, then there is no general duty to assist victims of rights violations by other nations.[5]

---

[5]There is one way in which a negative libertarian interpretation of civil rights might nonetheless support a duty to intervene: the negative liberty might give rise to a right to be free from any violation of one's rights, and not just a prohibition against violations by one's own state. Then, this negative liberty might obligate a government to take action against another government that was violating the negative liberty. Again, this justification requires an inquiry into the foundations supporting the liberty in the first place; do they support a conclusion that a government must take affirmative steps to protect the individual's right to be left alone?

Furthermore, if our policymakers would wish to assert affirmative duties as a basis for humanitarian intervention, they would have to show that these duties applied internationally as well as domestically. They would need a basis for recognizing that outsiders also have such rights; the foundations for the right to affirmative assistance would have to be common humanity or some other widely applicable rationale. Again, it is not clear that such a general duty to assist accords with our current philosophical intuitions. The United States has not recognized general affirmative duties to persons outside its borders. It does not recognize a general duty to provide economic assistance to outsiders on the basis of common humanity and at best has shown some mild general inclination to charity. How can it recognize general duties of assistance at the expense of other governments when it does not recognize them at its own expense? Why would we have a duty to help them emigrate but no duty to keep them from starving?

As citizens, of course, we need not be restrained by the positions of our current policymakers. We remain free to argue that there is a duty of humanitarian intervention in order to assist those in other nations. The general point remains, however, that to show such a duty we must address the existence of a general obligation of affirmative assistance. To make this argument, we must be prepared to recognize its implications both for domestic affairs and for other international issues. We must be prepared to assume an affirmative duty to prevent rights violations generally, accepting a theory of affirmative responsibilities that could conceivably prove inconvenient in a context where assumption of such duties was more costly.

The problem of humanitarian intervention thus combines many elements of domestic political theory. There is the question of the immunity of the victim-violator relationship from outside interference. If (as will happen under most political theories, one guesses) this relationship is not immune, then there is an issue of whether assistance may legitimately come from another *government*. The vertical thesis requires that coercion of the perpetrator be shown to be legitimate; this might be done either by showing some general right of all governments to enforce natural law or by establishing an obligation to assist the victims that itself provides a basis for action. The general enforceability of natural law must be applicable to domestic as well as international issues, as must general obligations of affirmative assistance. At each step in this inquiry there are difficult issues of domestic political theory. The vertical thesis only serves to formulate them, not to answer them.

Conclusion: Political Theory
for an Interdependent World

When asked at a debate at Oxford why American foreign policy was any more defensible than Soviet foreign policy, Casper Weinberger replied that American foreign policy could be changed by the American people.[1] Though one may doubt his empirical assumption[2] (especially in this age of covert actions), one is struck by the connection he drew between international relations and the domestic political theories that (in his view) motivate the superpowers. His defense of American foreign policy was in essence a defense of the American domestic method of decision making.

Weinberger was of course not the first foreign-policy expert to draw this connection. George Kennan had used the connection to a somewhat different purpose. Speaking of the Spanish-American War and its consequences, he noted the incongruity of a state organized internally as a democracy (the United States) but holding colonies internationally (the Philippines) that were not granted comparable

[1] Barton Gellman, "Oxford Letter: The Weinberger-Thompson Debate," *American Oxonian* 70 (Spring 1984): 115, 117.

[2] See, for instance, the conclusion that "free societies" are entirely capable of atrocities abroad in Noam Chomsky and Edward Herman, *The Political Economy of Human Rights*, vol. I: *The Washington Connection and Third World Fascism* (Boston, Mass.: South End Press, 1979).

democratic rights.[3] Here, the existence of domestic democracy was put to a critical use, namely, to question the legitimacy of our imperialistic aspirations. Yet although the conclusions drawn are quite at odds with each other, both Kennan and Weinberger perceived that our notions of domestic political legitimacy are somehow linked with justification of our foreign-policy decisions.

This link is, of course, the topic that we have been addressing. We have argued in a variety of contexts that domestic political theory can be usefully applied to problems of international affairs. For example, the current dispute over international distributive justice has addressed the question whether domestic theories of redistribution ought to be applied internationally. Similarly, the debate over international human rights asks (among other things) whether state sovereignty protects a state from outside intervention when it is acting in a fundamentally illegitimate way toward its own citizens. What these examples illustrate is the naturalness, the perfect ease, with which insights from domestic political analysis can be translated into international terms.

What they do not do, however, is explain how as a general matter fields that have usually been treated as separate ought to be related to one another. These examples involve scarcely more than selecting from political theory one or another argument whose relevance to international affairs is fairly obvious. While ad hoc reliance on selected arguments can provide insights, it is far short of what is really needed. What is really needed is a foundational understanding of when and why arguments from political theory are useful in analyzing international problems. According to the vertical thesis, arguments from political theory are relevant to international relations because they both deal with the same issue: the legitimacy of state power.

Having said this, we can see how Kennan's reasoning was more nearly right than Weinberger's in drawing implications from the democratic nature of the American system. If we consider the relationship between the United States and those in other countries who are adversely affected by our actions, it comes to seem almost en-

---

[3]George Kennan, *Realities of American Foreign Policy* (Princeton, N.J.: Princeton University Press, 1954), 47.

tirely irrelevant whether U.S. decisions are backed by U.S. voters. From the perspective of political theory, justification is owed to those whose lives are influenced by a decision. It is not enough simply to check a policy against the wishes of those who are allowed to vote. To select some group of persons, designate them the electorate, and then let them vote on an issue does not make the outcome ''democratic''. One might as well simply define the electorate *within the country* as all white, male, property owners, restrict the franchise to them, and call this arrangement democratic also. An important remaining question is the issue of whose views should matter in the first place.

Kennan's observation, when suitably expanded, provides needed insight into some current attitudes of other nations toward our foreign policies. It must be expanded because the argument cannot theoretically be limited to situations of formal territorial annexation. Other types of coercion also pose problems of legitimacy. The attitudes of the citizens of a country that is virtually completely dominated by another can easily be interpreted in terms that resonate with the American historical experience. Admittedly, modern accusations of ''imperialism'' and ''colonialism'' are often rhetorical excess. Nonetheless, one can better understand their appeal if one attempts sympathetically to compare the situation of powerless noncitizens to that of American colonists. In both cases, it should not be surprising that there is resentment against a distant government that makes self-interested decisions affecting one's life in important ways, without taking one's needs or preferences into account. It is not at all far-fetched for such a citizen to perceive an illegitimacy comparable to that perceived by the American colonists. This is a response that political theory ought to set out to understand and evaluate. Is such influence over outsiders justifiable or not? Is the resentment that it causes legitimate or unfounded?

Horizontal approaches sidestep this issue. So long as there is no official colonial relationship, there is a situation of formal sovereign equality. A vertical appraisal avoids the rhetoric of formal sovereign equality because it is simply not enough to say that states are equal to one another. The relevant question is whether they are behaving justly in their relations with one another's (as well as their own) citizens. Their sovereign equality may be beside the point where one state consistently coerces the other's citizens, but the converse is not also the case. We are missing an important element of the impact of our actions on people beyond our borders when we fail to inquire into the political legitimacy of our actions that have international consequences. We may decide, after taking a critical look, that all of our actions are in fact justified; and this conclusion may even be correct. At least the question will have been raised.

If international law needs the insights of political theory, political theory also needs the insights of international law. The usual approach to political legitimacy involves asking only about the relations between the state and its citizens. This may have been good enough in a time when the average person had connections with only one state. When Hobbes and Locke wrote, the prospect of coercion by a state other than one's own was not likely to arise in the minds of most citizens. Now that transborder interactions are common, owing to commercial activity and international travel (not to mention long-range weapons), the more complicated question of state coercion toward the world at large can no longer be postponed.

Political theories that addressed the legitimacy of a state's coercion of its own citizens are simply not adequate to the job of assessing the legitimacy of a state's coercion of outsiders. The usual touchstones of legitimacy—voting, for instance—are irrelevant to the visitor (who also is expected to respect local law) or to the outsider who, while remaining at home, nevertheless experiences the impact of a state's actions. When the United States supplies arms to revolutionaries in a third-world country, it has an impact on noncitizens, as it does when it devalues its currency or decides not to provide famine relief or reschedule a debt. Talk of ''consent'' or ''voting'' is simply not relevant in evaluating the legitimacy of such actions.

It would therefore be worse than disingenuous to suggest that one can simply take existing theories of political obligation and apply them mechanically to problems of international relations. First, it is clear that legitimacy and obligation are not monolithic; there may be a variety of types of coercion that are legitimate under a variety of different cirumstances. Drafting an individual into the armed services is different from simply requiring him or her to obey traffic laws or to pay a sales tax. The sufficiency of a purported justification for state coercion may depend on the extent of the power that the state asserts. To some degree, then, one must differentiate between the types of state power exercised. Legitimacy may mean different things in different contexts, and in cases where nonmembers are simply subject to different sorts of state coercion than members are, the coercion of nonmembers may have to be justified in different terms.

In addition to providing a more refined conception of the various state powers that must be justified, political theory must address more thoroughly the problem of territoriality. Too often, purported justifications of state authority proceed as though political theory dealt simply with relations between individuals and the political institutions that they create. Political theory is for and about human beings. This approach overlooks the way in which political relationships are mediated through access to land. Membership is defined largely by where one lives; consent is inferred from a person's entering into a geographical space; and so forth. Thus a political theory must explain how territorial boundaries arise. It must explain sovereignty over land as well as people. It is not enough to spell out the relevant substantive rights and procedural limitations on how decisions are made because these points cannot explain which of many possible fair institutions deserves one's support. The problem of justifying boundaries includes difficult questions about how seriously to take the status quo. When we try to justify political obligation, do we try to justify the obligation of an individual to his or her own current state? If so, are we therefore treating the existing configuration of nation states as part of the institution that we seek to justify? And if the answer is yes (it usually seems to be), then why in the world should we assume that the existing pattern of obligations is justifiable? Have we defined the problem so that it has no solution?

Other important issues remain. A domestic political theory must specify which are the coercive actions that must be politically justified. Some activities are recognized as official state activities and others are not. A theory must, in other words, supply definitional as well as evaluative criteria for state action. What activities do we recognize as official in the sense of being subject to the requirement of political justification? What harms count as political acts?

Finally, a political theory has to take a position on the question of affirmative obligations to assist necessitous individuals. Is it always defensible merely to leave people alone? Moreover, the rationale for its position is crucial. Does the rationale apply to all persons in need simply because they are persons? Or only to some persons? Is there a reason to believe that it differentiates between insiders and persons not subject to a state's coercive power?

The demands that the vertical approach places on domestic political theory are therefore quite astounding. Vertical analysis, clearly, is not for the philosophically faint of heart. It might seem for this reason that the vertical thesis is, in reality, no more than a high-level exercise in buck-passing. Take an intractable problem of international law; redefine it as an intractable problem of domestic political theory; and then pass it on to a political philosopher to solve.

There is, perhaps, something to this accusation. We have raised far more questions about domestic political theory in these pages than we have answered. Time and again, extremely difficult issues were simply pointed out as the analogs of issues that domestic political philosophers do, or should, address. At such points, we have stated merely that the vertical thesis holds that the question should be analyzed in the same way as its domestic analog. As a matter of international law, the problem disappears.

Yet, there is more to it than that. To say that something is an issue of political philosophy is to impose a consistency constraint on it; and doing so is the main function of the vertical approach. It doesn't matter who solves such a problem. Political philosophers are accustomed to dealing with questions of this nature, but international lawyers are welcome to try their hand as well. The point, in fact, is that with regard to the analysis of jurisdictional boundaries, academic specialization has done far more harm than good. The vertical thesis holds that political theory and international relations are not isolated academic specialties that can be discussed without reference to each other. Simply ending the artificial isolation between the disciplines would result in a significant change in the ways we think about the two sets of problems. The international consequences of political theories are an important and appropriate topic for lawyers, political scientists, and philosophers alike.

Index

Library of Congress Cataloging-in-Publication Data

Brilmayer, Lea.
    Justifying international acts/Lea Brilmayer.
        p.   cm.
    Includes index.
    ISBN 0–8014–2278–7
    1. International law.   2. Duress (International law)
    3. Jurisdiction, Territorial.   I. Title.
    JX3110.B675J87   1989
    341–dc20   89–7121